Wonderful
WORLD 6
WORKBOOK

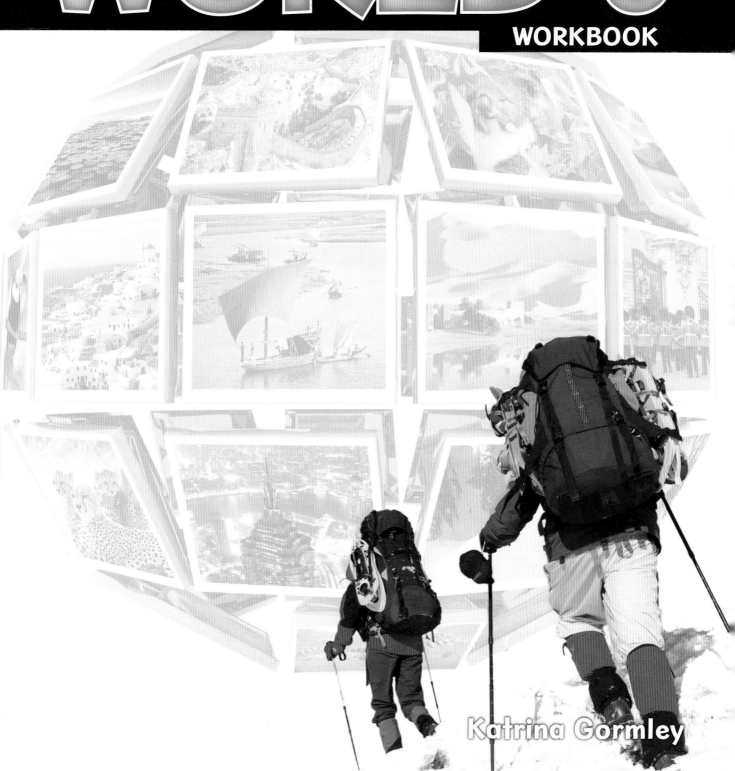

Katrina Gormley

Wonderful World 6 Workbook
Katrina Gormley

Publisher: Jason Mann
Director of Content Development: Sarah Bideleux
Commissioning Editor: Carol Goodwright
Development Editor: Lynn Thomson
Assistant Editor: Manuela Barros
Project Editor: Amy Smith
Production Controller: Tom Relf
Art Director: Natasa Arsenidou
Cover designer: Sophia Ioannidou
Text designer: Tania Diakaki, Dora Danasi
Compositor: Rouli Manias
National Geographic Editorial Liaison: Leila Hishmeh

Acknowledgements
Illustrated by Spyros Kontis

The publisher would like to thank the following sources for permission to reproduce their copyright protected photos:
Cover: left to right, top to bottom: (Jim Richardson/ National Geographic), (George Steinmetz/National Geographic), (Medford Taylor/National Geographic), (David Edwards/National Geographic), (Eduardo Rivero/Shutterstock Images), (Richard Nowitz/National Geographic), (Dick Durrance II/National Geographic), (Guy Needham/National Geographic), (Scott S. Warren/National Geographic), (Michael Poliza/National Geographic), (Fritz Hoffmann/National Geographic), main image (Kapu/Shutterstock).
Inside: Dreamstime LLC – pp29 (Ankevanwyk), 36 (Pitrs10), 96 (Demonike), 97 (Alenavlad); National Geographic Stock – pp22 (O. Louis Mazzatenta), 40 (Bill Hatcher), 94 (Gordon Wiltsie), 112; Shutterstock – pp24 (Tomasz Bidermann), 25br (Geoffrey Kuchera); Thinkstock – pp4 (iStockphoto), 46 (iStockphoto), 51 (Photos.com), 55bc (iStockphoto), 58 (iStockphoto), 68 (iStockphoto), 71 (iStockphoto), 91 (iStockphoto), 97 (PhotoObjects.net). All other photos courtesy of Shutterstock.

ISBN: 978-1-111-40249-5

National Geographic Learning
Cheriton House
North Way
Andover
Hampshire
SP10 5BE
United Kingdom

Cengage Learning is a leading provider of customized learning solutions with office locations around the globe, including Singapore, the United Kingdom, Australia, Mexico, Brazil and Japan. Locate your local office at: **international.cengage.com/region**

Cengage Learning products are represented in Canada by Nelson Education, Ltd.

Visit National Geographic Learning online at **ngl.cengage.com**
Visit our corporate website at **www.cengage.com**

Printed in Greece by Bakis SA
Print Number 05 Print Year 2016

Contents

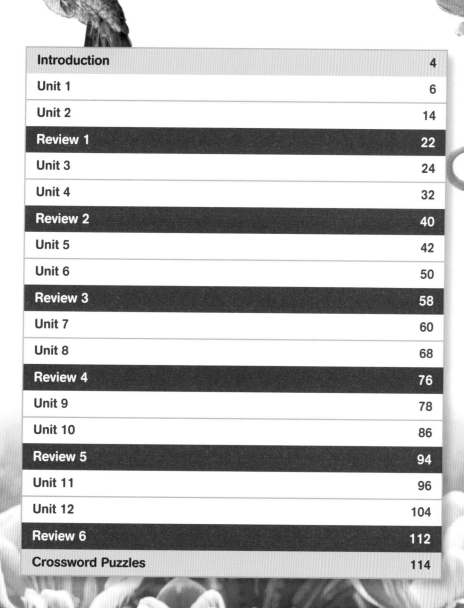

A Find four countable and four uncountable nouns and complete the sentences.

```
W  A  P  P  L  I  C  A  T  I  O  N
E  C  O  F  F  E  E  S  D  Q  P  M
I  N  F  O  R  M  A  T  I  O  N  S
G  P  U  S  A  B  I  W  F  L  P  C
H  C  R  O  F  D  V  X  F  I  A  M
T  P  N  U  D  C  B  I  E  V  F  O
H  U  I  L  C  U  S  E  R  E  E  O
G  R  T  G  H  Y  I  J  E  S  I  F
W  S  U  V  T  C  A  S  N  P  N  M
Q  C  R  U  I  K  K  W  C  O  R  T
D  R  E  S  A  Y  I  W  E  N  I  H
I  E  S  U  I  T  C  A  S  E  L  L
```

1 How many ___differences___ are there between these two pictures?

2 Would you like a cup of _____?

3 Is this your job _____ ?

4 She bought lots of new _____ for her house.

5 The _____ of this bag is ten kilos.

6 The website's got lots of _____ on this species.

7 His clothes fitted into one _____ .

8 Do you like _____ on pizza?

B Circle the correct words.

1 I'd love a can / (cup) of coffee.

2 How many bottles / glasses of ketchup did you buy?

3 She's eating a bowl / jar of noodles and vegetables.

4 Can you get a can / cup of beans from the supermarket?

5 Shall I order the kids a glass / bowl of orange juice?

6 Put the lid back on the bowl / jar, please.

C Underline each word in the correct colour.

adjective

adverb   article   modal

noun   preposition

pronoun   verb

1 The students entered the classroom noisily yesterday.

2 Can we take a break now?

3 Give the book to your partner.

4 A quiet boy sat in the playground.

5 My aunt is very tall.

6 She couldn't open the heavy door.

D Complete the sentences with these words.

| adjective | adverb | article | modal verb | noun | preposition | pronoun | verb |

1 A(n) _____noun_____ is a person, place or thing.
2 A(n) _____ expresses an action or state.
3 A(n) _____ is used before a noun to show place, time, etc.
4 A(n) _____ describes a noun.
5 A(n) _____ is definite or indefinite.
6 A(n) _____ is a verb used with another verb.
7 A(n) _____ adds information to a verb or adjective.
8 A(n) _____ is used instead of a noun.

E Complete the pairs of sentences with the words given.

1 your   you're
   a   Is this _____your_____ coffee?
   b   _____ driving too fast!

2 its   it's
   a   Give the kitten _____ food!
   b   _____ a lovely, sunny day today.

3 may be   maybe
   a   _____ I'll cut the grass later on.
   b   She _____ a little late home this evening.

4 their   they're
   a   _____ always complaining about the service.
   b   That's _____ new car in the garage.

5 who's   whose
   a   That's the man _____ wife had an accident.
   b   Do you know _____ bringing olives to the party?

Vocabulary

A Circle the odd one out.

1	routine	(goals)	steps
2	contestant	competition	achievement
3	impressive	admirable	firm
4	key	tip	advice
5	succeed	audition	achieve
6	miserable	lousy	relevant

B Find eight fame-related words and use them to complete the sentences.

M	A	R	U	C	E	L	B	D	M	I
N	R	A	N	R	C	N	L	E	P	I
P	O	T	N	H	I	T	M	T	O	M
A	B	T	X	I	A	E	V	E	S	P
D	M	E	A	S	U	R	E	R	P	R
M	I	N	U	U	S	T	T	M	P	E
I	F	T	D	C	B	S	E	I	A	S
R	O	I	I	C	X	L	R	N	O	S
A	(P	O	T	E	N	T	I	A	L)	I
T	Q	N	I	D	A	N	I	T	M	O
I	M	P	E	S	S	I	O	I	V	N
O	D	M	I	R	E	T	P	O	S	P
N	A	U	D	I	T	I	O	N	R	A

1 The young star has got a lot of ____potential____ and will do well.

2 The YaYa's new song is a big _____ all over the world.

3 Did the star make a good _____ on you?

4 Mark went for an _____ for a Hollywood film.

5 The judges are full of _____ for the young performers.

6 It takes a lot of _____ to get to the top.

7 What is the true _____ of success?

8 Some stars do anything to get other people's _____ .

C Complete the dialogue with these words.

achievable   determined   focus on   ~~hard~~   stand out   work out

Interviewer: Sam, you're a famous judge on the UK's most popular talent show. Have you got any good advice for young people with stars in their eyes?

Sam: Well, firstly I'd like to say that the road to success is a (1) _____hard_____ one. Stars are usually very (2) _____ people and constantly (3) _____ their strengths and try to improve. Success only comes to people who can (4) _____ what their real goals are.

Interviewer: What is the best way for young celebrities to (5) _____ in a crowd?

Sam: I think the main thing is to have (6) _____ goals. That way success is more likely.

Grammar

A Complete the sentences with the correct form of the Present Simple or the Present Continuous of these verbs.

compete   make   not live   not smile   shout   start   watch   ~~work~~

1 We _____ are working _____ on a new dance routine today.
2 _____ you always _____ X Factor?
3 That annoying actress _____ forever _____ at her manager.
4 They _____ time every day to practise singing.
5 _____ Don _____ in this year's *Rising Stars* competition?
6 Millionaires _____ in this town.
7 The star _____ in this picture. She looks sad.
8 What time _____ the concert _____ ?

B Write T (true) or F (false).

1 He enjoys listening to her play.   F
2 They aren't looking at each other.   ☐
3 They don't enjoy rehearsing.   ☐
4 He likes music.   ☐
5 She never wins competitions.   ☐
6 She sometimes pretends to be a star.   ☐

C Choose the correct answers.

1 I go to rehearsals _____ .
   (a) three times a week
   b   never
   c   at the moment

2 _____ tonight?
   a   Is the star singing
   b   Does the star sing
   c   The star sings

3 The band isn't touring _____ .
   a   regularly
   b   for the time being
   c   on Saturdays

4 Those fans are _____ asking for my autograph!
   a   never
   b   sometimes
   c   constantly

5 _____ they practising for the concert?
   a   Are
   b   Do
   c   Is

6 The star always goes to Alexandria _____ August.
   a   in
   b   on
   c   at

Vocabulary

A Circle the correct words.

1   I can't believe the band are splitting / snapping up!
2   Gina always pays / fetches an arm and a leg for theatre memorabilia.
3   Robbie Williams has got a successful spare / solo career.
4   What time does the group come on display / stage?
5   The actor is heading for / over his car.
6   That writer likes to be in the public ear / eye.

B Complete the crossword.

Across

1   The memorabilia is on _____ to an American museum at the moment.
3   He's rich, but he doesn't spend lots of money; he isn't _____ .
5   I prefer _____ clothes to modern ones.
7   Wow! The actress looks _____ in that red dress.
8   He isn't in a band now, but he is the _____ singer of *Hanging Garden*.

Down

2   It's _____ how much some people spend on silly things.
4   How much are you _____ to pay for the tickets?
6   Is that a _____ autograph? That's amazing.

C Complete the sentences.

| auction | cash | glimpse | memorabilia | paintwork | track |

1   What is your favourite _____track_____ on the new CD?
2   Did you get a _____ of the actor going into that shop?
3   This car has got very unusual _____ .
4   Not many people turned up at the _____ .
5   Don't carry so much _____ when you go out.
6   This restaurant has got lots of Hollywood _____ on display.

Grammar

A Look at the picture and write sentences with the Present Simple or the Present Continuous.

1 the band / appear / in concert
   The band is appearing in concert.

2 the men in the band / have / guitars
   _____

3 they / not play / keyboards
   _____

4 they / wear / black clothes
   _____

5 the fans / like / the performance
   _____

B Circle the correct words.

1 The bank manager never forgets / is never forgetting his rich customers.

2 What are you thinking / do you think of the play?

3 We're seeing / see the performance at 3 o'clock this afternoon.

4 Some fans feel / are feeling the tickets are too expensive.

5 We aren't having / don't have a party after this year's premiere.

6 The famous chef's cooking tastes / is tasting great.

7 Who does this Bentley belonging / belong to?

8 Nobody doubts / is doubting that she'll become famous.

C Complete the email with the correct form of the Present Simple or the Present Continuous of the verbs in brackets.

⬤ ⬤ ⬤	Email

New   Reply   Forward   Print   Delete   Send & Receive

Hi Jerry,

How (1) _____are you feeling_____ (feel) this morning? Mark says you felt unwell after your audition yesterday. I hope you're better today. I'm sure the judges will pick you to be on the show because you're a great singer.

I (2) _____ (not want) to bother you, but I have a question. (3) _____ you _____ (remember) that *Coldplay* DVD I lent you? (4) _____ you _____ (think) I could have it back? I really need it for this weekend. You know how much I (5) _____ (love) *Coldplay*. Mark and I (6) _____ (think) of doing one of their songs for our audition next week. Gary (7) _____ (not agree) with us, so I hope the DVD will change his mind. I (8) _____ (not understand) why he doesn't like their songs, do you?

That's all for the moment. Take care,

Les

9

Vocabulary

Complete the words.

1 This is someone who takes part in a competition.   c o n t e s t a n t
2 This is someone's signature.   a _ _ _ _ _ _ _ _ _
3 This is someone who hasn't got parents.   o _ _ _ _ _ _
4 This is a very wealthy person.   m _ _ _ _ _ _ _ _ _ _
5 This is the person an actor plays.   c _ _ _ _ _ _ _ _ _
6 These are objects that belonged to celebrities.   m _ _ _ _ _ _ _ _ _ _
7 This is an object with a star's signature on it.   s _ _ _ _ _ c _ _ _
8 This is where you can buy expensive objects.   a _ _ _ _ _ _

Listening

A 🎧 **Do the quiz, then listen and check your answers.**

1 On which show does actress Miley Cyrus play the character Miley Stewart?
   a High School Musical
   b Hannah Montana *(circled)*
   c The X-Factor

2 Which of these famous actresses hasn't adopted an orphan?
   a Angelina Jolie
   b Victoria Beckham
   c Madonna

3 Which blockbuster film cost $300 million to produce?
   a Pirates of the Caribbean: At World's End
   b 2012
   c Quantum of Solace

4 Which famous singer has got two dogs called Bearlie and Bella?
   a Chris Martin
   b Snoop Dogg
   c Justin Timberlake

5 Which famous person started her career on the Mickey Mouse Club?
   a Britney Spears
   b Gwyneth Paltrow
   c Lady Gaga

B 🎧 **Listen to the announcement for an auction and complete the notes.**

Crystal's Memorabilia Auctions

Message services

Press 1 for information about auctions in
   (1) _____June_____ .
Press 2 for a Guide to Auctions.
Press 3 for future auctions.
Press 4 to (2) _____ to an assistant.

Auctions in June

(3) _____ toys: 5th June at 6.30 pm
Tickets cost (4) _____
Cars: 11th June at 11.00 am
Includes copies of cars used in
(5) _____ and films
Autograph Auction: 23rd June at 5.30 pm
Includes (6) _____ objects such as
books, photos, CDs and DVDs, etc
Entrance free

Speaking

A Look at the pictures and write M (man), G (girl) or B (both).

Remember!

When we are talking about people we use expressions like these.
It/He/She looks like ...
It/He/She seems/appears to be + -ing ...
I (don't) think/believe/imagine he/she ...
He is wearing/looking at/playing ...

1

2

1	rehearsing	M	6	cap
2	sailing		7	belt
3	playing a part		8	costume
4	long hair		9	weapons
5	beard		10	casual clothes

B Complete the sentences about the people in the photos above.

1 The man looks like _he's rehearsing for a film or TV programme_   .

2 He appears to be _____ .

3 I imagine he _____ .

4 He's wearing _____ .

5 The girl looks like _____ .

6 She seems to be _____ .

7 I think she _____ .

8 She's wearing _____ .

C Work with a partner and take it in turns to describe what you can see in the pictures. Student A should talk about picture 1 and Student B should talk about picture 2.

Discussion

'It's easy to be happy when you're rich.' Discuss.

Vocabulary

Choose the correct answers.

1 The film was so _____ I laughed from beginning to end.
   a exciting
   b impressive
   c hilarious

2 Kim's writing the _____ for a new TV series at the moment.
   a storyline
   b cast
   c set

3 The book was so _____ I guessed the ending immediately.
   a predictable
   b entertaining
   c original

4 The actor's _____ was brilliant.
   a hit
   b plot
   c performance

5 My favourite _____ was the car chase.
   a scene
   b scenery
   c character

6 I get scared easily so I don't like _____ .
   a dramas
   b comedies
   c thrillers

Remember!

Always be clear about the register you should use before you begin writing.

postcards, emails, friendly letters ➡ informal language
reviews, articles ➡ semi-formal language
job applications and letters of complaint ➡ formal language

Model writing task

A Read the writing task and the model review and underline the sentences that are too informal.

Your school magazine wants to publish reviews of films school students recommend. Write a review of a film you want to recommend to other students. Describe what happens in the film and discuss two reasons why you recommend it.

B Now write the correct paragraph number (2-5) in the boxes to show which informal sentences a-d replace.

a It's an entertaining film that appeals to young people. ☐ 5

b The result is an interesting drama mixed with music and dance. ☐

c One of the reasons I recommend the film is the acting. ☐

d These include problems growing up and making decisions about what to do when they leave school. ☐

model composition

High School Musical 3: Senior Year

Are you looking for an entertaining way to spend your evening? Then watch *High School Musical 3: Senior Year*.

The film is a comedy and a drama as well as a musical. The storyline is about a group of high school students in their final year. The students face the usual difficulties that final year high school students face. It's all stuff like not knowing what to do and that kind of thing.

Check out the acting. The main actors are Zac Efron (Troy), Vanessa Hudgens (Gabriella) and Ashley Tisdale (Sharpay). In general, the three stars give impressive performances. Their singing and dancing make the film exciting and shows how talented they are.

Another reason for recommending the film is its plot. The director Kenny Ortega has very successfully mixed the story of their friendships with Sharpay's attempt to create a great end-of-year show. It's cool how there's acting and dancing together.

I recommend *High School Musical 3* to others without any doubt. It's totally fab for teenagers.

Grammar

A Circle the correct words.

1 They're showing the directors the new theatre / the new theatre the directors.
2 Did you sell the memorabilia to the millionaire / to the millionaire the memorabilia?
3 Give the singer this magazine / this magazine the singer.
4 She's writing for our website a review / a review for our website.
5 Send Jim the tickets / the tickets Jim tomorrow.
6 Offer the audience a refund / a refund the audience.

B Put the words in the correct order to make sentences.

1 give / DVD / please / copy / me / a / signed / of / the
   Please give me a signed copy of the DVD.

2 the / watch / silence / film / in
   _____

3 celebrity / don't / take / of / photographs / the
   _____

4 the / to / band / director / showing / their / are / dance routine / the
   _____

5 Fergus / to / lent / you / his / guitar
   _____

6 ?/ did / book / seats / for / the / whole / enough / group / you
   _____

Your writing task

A Read the writing task and the model review and tick (✓) the boxes to show which points you will include in your review. Then complete the plan.

Your school magazine wants to publish reviews of films school students don't recommend. Write a review about a film you disliked. Describe what happens in the film and discuss two features that disappointed you.

a Describe what happens in the film. ☑
b Discuss another feature that disappointed you. ☐
c Discuss one feature that disappointed you. ☐
d Discuss the kind of films you prefer. ☐
e Introduce the film you are going to write about and briefly say why you didn't like it. ☐
f Sum up your opinion of the film and recommend students not to watch it. ☐

Paragraph 1: _e_
Paragraph 2: _____
Paragraph 3: _____
Paragraph 4: _____
Paragraph 5: _____

B Now write your review.

Vocabulary

A Write P (Person), G (Group) or O (Object).

1 scroll   `O`
2 curator
3 trunk
4 fleet
5 society
6 admiral
7 ancestor
8 portrait

B Match.

1 Did he really come
2 Nobody uttered
3 George's face went
4 When did the Neolithic period come
5 Does your society approve
6 Napoleon came

a as white as a sheet.
b of women working?
c a sound in the museum.
d to power in 1804.
e face to face with a tiger?
f to an end?

C Choose the correct answers.

1 You look really _____ . Don't you understand the article?
   a uneasy
   b puzzled
   c speechless

2 It came as no _____ the children were bored at the natural history museum.
   a way
   b amazement
   c surprise

3 The curator _____ it was the new assistant's fault that the exhibit broke.
   a suspected
   b traded
   c echoed

4 Visiting the pyramids was a(n) _____ come true.
   a dream
   b permission
   c appointment

5 Ask the _____ at the front door when the museum closes.
   a journalist
   b guard
   c actor

6 The door banged shut _____ .
   a unfortunately
   b eerily
   c exactly

Grammar

A Complete the sentences with the correct form of the Past Simple or the Past Continuous of the verbs in brackets.

1 While Murray _____was working_____ (work) at the newspaper, he wrote an article about mummies.
2 Dad _____ (read) about ancient history and Mum was watching the news.
3 The ship _____ (sink) in 1899.
4 The history lesson _____ (become) more and more boring every minute.
5 When _____ the first car crash _____ (take place)?
6 He arrived at the school, _____ (head for) the history department and started shouting at the teacher.

B Answer the questions.

1 Where did your ancestors come from?

_____

2 What were you doing at this time two days ago?

_____

3 How did you feel during your last history test?

_____

4 What job did your great-grandfather do?

_____

5 What were you wearing on your seventh birthday?

_____

6 Who took you to school when you were younger?

_____

C Complete the paragraph with the correct form of the Past Simple or the Past Continuous of these verbs.

come   look   make   not have on
not seem   snow   stay   wear

'Oh no, it's that strange girl again! I really don't understand her. She (1) _____came_____ here last winter and she (2) _____ for three hours. She (3) _____ at me the whole time and she (4) _____ to get bored. It (5) _____ me feel a bit uneasy. At least this time she's got warm clothes on. The last time it (6) _____ and she (7) _____ winter clothes. She (8) _____ a T-shirt and jeans. I really don't know why she likes me so much. I guess she likes old statues.'

Vocabulary

A Look at the pictures and write the correct words.

inhabitants   remains   settlement   ~~visible~~   winding

1 _____visible_____   2 _____   3 _____

4 _____   5 _____

B Write the missing letters.

1 People do this when they go to live in another place.   m i g r a t e
2 This is a period of a thousand years.   m _ _ _ _ _ _ _ _
3 You do this when you say a theory is true.   c _ _ _ _ _ _
4 This is where people can meet to talk, eat or have fun.   g _ _ _ _ _ _ _ _ p _ _ _ _
5 We do this when we connect one thing to another in our minds. a _ _ _ _ _ _ _ _ w _ _ _
6 This is all the cultural things we get from our ancestors.   h _ _ _ _ _ _ _

C Circle the correct words.

1 Their theory isn't paid / (based) on evidence.
2 The winter of 1848 was very preserved / harsh in our country.
3 The Potato Famine resulted in / to many people migrating from Ireland.
4 My great-grandmother faced / passed away in 1960.
5 How many layers / outlines of earth were covering the houses?

Grammar

A Complete the sentences with used to, didn't use to or would. Sometimes more than one answer
is possible.

1 My grandfather walked six miles to school every day because there _____*didn't use to*_____ be school buses.

2 In the ancient world, people _____ meet to trade at oases.

3 I always _____ feel really bored in school history lessons.

4 Neolithic people didn't have metal. They _____ make things out of stone.

5 People _____ be very afraid of pirates in the past.

6 When Sam was young, she _____ visit the Natural History Museum once a year.

7 They _____ have computers two hundred years ago.

8 The villagers _____ help each other when they were in trouble.

B Choose the correct answers.

1 Did the ancient Peruvians _____ build pyramids?
   a would
   b use to *(circled)*
   c used to

2 Three centuries ago people _____ have cars.
   a didn't use
   b wouldn't
   c didn't use to

3 Families _____ sit round the fire in the evenings.
   a use to
   b would
   c used

4 Charles Dickens used _____ stories.
   a write
   b to write
   c wrote

5 My great-grandmother _____ live in Mumbai.
   a used to
   b use to
   c would

6 There _____ to be horses in Australia but there are now.
   a used
   b would
   c didn't use

C Write what many Neolithic people did or didn't do. Use used to, didn't use to or would. Sometimes
more than one answer is possible.

1 live in caves ✗
   They didn't use to live in caves.

2 play computer games ✗
   _____

3 sleep on stone beds ✓
   _____

4 eat fish ✓
   _____

5 go to school ✗
   _____

6 have community meetings ✓
   _____

Vocabulary

Complete the sentences with these words.

excavation   exhibition   expert   finds   fossil   ~~refreshments~~   scroll   skeleton

1   There are _____*refreshments*_____ in the café.
2   Wasn't your grandmother a(n) _____ on mummies?
3   This _____ is temporary and will be on display until next month.
4   How many bones are there in a dinosaur _____ ?
5   We found a(n) _____ of a strange animal in a stone.
6   I'd love to go on an archaeological _____ .
7   Can the museum keep all the _____ from this site?
8   What does it say on that _____ ?

Listening

A 🎧 **Listen and number the pictures in the correct order.**

a

b

c [1]

d

e

f

B 🎧 **Listen to a conversation between Hannah and Rob. Decide whether each statement is right (A) or wrong (B).**

1   At the beginning, Hannah is on the phone.   [A]
2   Hannah doesn't think it's a good idea for them to visit the museum today.   [ ]
3   Rob suggests that they take his father with them.   [ ]
4   Rob's dad will explore the whole museum.   [ ]
5   Only two children will like the dinosaur skeletons.   [ ]
6   At first, Rob suggests arriving at the museum at 9.00.   [ ]

Speaking

Remember!

When we open discussions in speaking tasks, we use phrases like these.
Let's begin/start by looking at ...
First of all, ...
To begin with, ...

When we explain the choices we have made in speaking tasks, we use phrases like these.
I don't think/believe ... is important/helpful because ...
He/She/We/They shouldn't ... because ...
It's a good idea/not such a good idea to ... because ...
It'd be better to ... /if he/she ... because ...

A Look at the Speaking task in C and tick (✓) the things you think are useful for students.

library with history books ☐

film equipment and historical DVDs ☐

class trips to museums ☐

class trips to archaeological digs ☐

computer equipment and educational CD-ROMS ☐

B Use phrases from the *Remember!* box to complete this dialogue. Sometimes more than one answer is possible.

Dina: (1) _____ Let's begin _____ by discussing how useful the five choices are.

Joanne: Fine. (2) _____ the library with history books is very useful for the students. They won't have time to read all these books and they probably don't need them for their lessons.

Dina: I agree. These books are for experts. Also, (3) _____ spend the money on film equipment and DVDs because the students will get bored watching these kinds of films.

Joanne: But they will learn a lot from the films.

Dina: They will learn some things, but (4) _____ buy computer equipment and CD-ROMS because students can use these facilities whenever they need specific information.

Joanne: Yes, you are right. Most students know how to look for information on computers these days and they will be popular with all classes.

Dina: (5) _____ use the money on trips to museums because schools usually take students to museums anyway.

Joanne: Yes, and they're normally not interesting enough for the students so they don't learn anything. But (6) _____ for them to take classes on trips to archaeological excavations because they can learn a lot about history from the finds at the sites and they don't usually have the opportunity to visit these places.

C Your school history department is going to receive some extra money from a local historical society. They want it to be spent on things which will help students learn history. Look at the pictures below and discuss with your partner what the best two ways to spend the money are.

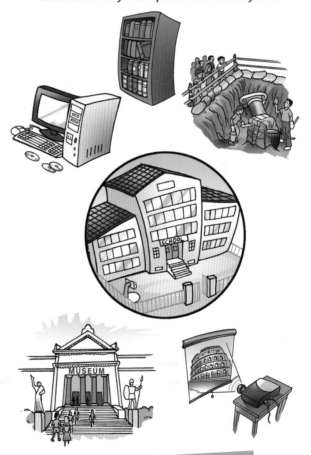

Discussion

'History is one of the most important school subjects.' Discuss.

Vocabulary

Write **SO** (Stating your opinion), **GE** (Giving more examples), **CC** (Comparing/Contrasting) or **C** (Concluding).

1 However, `CC`
2 Moreover, ☐
3 To my mind, ☐
4 To sum up, ☐
5 In my opinion, ☐

6 In addition, ☐
7 Furthermore, ☐
8 In conclusion, ☐
9 On the other hand, ☐
10 In my view, ☐

> ## Remember!
>
> Each paragraph in an essay has a topic sentence. The topic sentence usually comes at the beginning of the paragraph and tells us what the paragraph is about. It is then followed by supporting sentences which give examples of its main idea.

Model writing task

Read the writing task and the model essay and complete the essay with the correct sentences.

'Life was more difficult in the past.' Write an essay based on this statement and say whether you agree or disagree with the opinion it expresses.

a   On the other hand, some people argue that life was much easier in the past.

b   To sum up, I don't think life in the past was easier than it is today.

c   Many people feel that life in the past was much more difficult than it is today.

d   In my opinion, the people who say that life was better in the past are wrong.

model composition

(1) __c__ They point out that in the past people didn't use to have cars so they used to walk great distances. This was very tiring and meant that people couldn't travel very far. Also, people had to hunt for food in the distant past. For those of us who are used to getting our food from shops and supermarkets, this seems a very difficult way of life.

(2) _____ They say that there weren't as many problems and that life was simpler and better. They argue that people had fewer things but they were happier. Moreover, they say that our ancestors lived in close communities and all the members helped each other.

(3) _____ People's lives may have been simpler, but the conditions they lived in were very tough and they didn't have enough food or nice homes to live in.

(4) _____ People's everyday lives were simple and they only cared about their basic needs, but they were very poor and most of them had to live in terrible conditions.

Grammar

A **Circle the correct words.**

1 I can't (get)/ be used to our new history teacher.
2 Are you used / Did you use to work at the dinosaur exhibition?
3 Our ancestors were used to hunting / hunt for food.
4 The archaeologist is / gets used to working in bad weather.
5 It took people time to get use / used to cars.
6 I'm not / didn't used to reading history books.

B **Match.**

1 I used to
2 Did your grandmother
3 Salah al-Din soon got
4 The Egyptians were used
5 Is the museum curator
6 At Skara Brae, people

a use to have a computer?
b used to fighting.
c used to so many visitors?
d have a CD ROM about ancient civilizations.
e used to build stone houses.
f to seeing pyramids.

Your writing task

A **Read the writing task and number the points in the correct order to make a plan for your essay.**

'In the past, people used to help each other more than they do today.' Write an essay based on this statement and say whether you agree or disagree with the opinion it expresses.

a Present and analyse the arguments for the statement. ☐
b Come to a conclusion and express your opinion. ☐
c Introduce and rephrase the statement in the task. 1
d Present and analyse the arguments against the statement. ☐

B **Now write your essay.**

Reading

A Read the text about unusual archaeological finds.

Guarding China's first emperor

In 1974, some Chinese farmers were digging a well when they hit something hard. They kept digging and the head of a statue soon became visible. The farmers realised they were digging an important archaeological site.

It wasn't long before archaeologists came to work on the site. Their work resulted in one of the most unusual and impressive archaeological finds being uncovered. They removed more than a thousand life-sized statues of soldiers from the ground. The soldiers were ready for war and even held weapons. Some had horses with them.

The place where the farmers were digging was actually where Qin Shi Huangdi, China's first emperor, was buried. The soldiers were made and buried with the emperor to protect him on his journey after death. That was over 2,000 years ago.

When he was alive, emperor Qin Shi Huangdi was a powerful leader. His armies succeeded in bringing many regions together to make China one country. He was a very harsh leader, but always tried to do great things. In fact, Qin Shi Huangdi started the Great Wall of China.

During later excavations of the site, archaeologists discovered that Qin Shi Huangdi didn't only have statues of soldiers to guard him. There were also statues of servants, musicians and animals to serve and entertain him after his death. Archaeologists haven't uncovered the whole site yet but they think there may be as many as 7,000 statues still under the ground.

Almost four decades after the discovery of the site, some of the soldiers are on the move. In November 2009, they appeared in an exhibition in the National Geographic Museum in the US. Who knows, you may come face to face with them in a museum near you one day!

B Answer the questions.

1 What were the Chinese farmers doing when they found a statue?   *They were digging a well.*

2 What were the statues of soldiers carrying? _____

3 When did the first emperor of China die? _____

4 What did Qin Shi Huangdi and his armies manage to do? _____

5 What else did archaeologists discover at the site apart from soldiers? _____

6 Why did some of the statues of soldiers go to the US in 2009? _____

Vocabulary

Choose the correct answers.

1   The band's greatest _____ are on this special CD!
    a   finds
    b   theories
    c   hits

2   A _____ is a period of a thousand years.
    a   millionaire
    b   millennium
    c   memorabilia

3   How much did you _____ for that designer bag?
    a   compete
    b   pay
    c   approve

4   We found a _____ of a snail yesterday.
    a   fossil
    b   relic
    c   ruin

5   How many _____ lived in this village?
    a   communities
    b   inhabitants
    c   skeletons

6   The star refused to give me his _____ .
    a   layer
    b   premiere
    c   autograph

7   She looks very _____ in her new dress.
    a   well-known
    b   glamorous
    c   lousy

8   When did the Chinese emperor pass _____?
    a   away
    b   for
    c   with

9   The museum has an exhibition of _____ clothes this month.
    a   determined
    b   vintage
    c   hard

10 I didn't expect so many people to _____ up for the concert.
    a   turn
    b   snap
    c   split

11 The celebrity gave most of her money to _____ .
    a   settlement
    b   routine
    c   charity

12 The film is based _____ a true story.
    a   in
    b   to
    c   on

Grammar

Choose the correct answers.

1   Is he _____ to the premiere tonight?
    a   going
    b   go
    c   goes

2   Their new song _____ fantastic.
    a   is sounding
    b   sounds
    c   sounding

3   Bring _____ of the curator's contract.
    a   me a copy
    b   a copy me
    c   to me a copy

4   The dancer _____ her leg on stage last night.
    a   was breaking
    b   breaks
    c   broke

5   My aunt _____ to be at the same school as Dina.
    a   would
    b   used
    c   use

6   The young star can't get used _____ famous.
    a   to being
    b   be
    c   to be

7   Those fans _____ outside the recording studio.
    a   are always waiting
    b   are waiting always
    c   always are waiting

8   The actress _____ the new perfume right now.
    a   smells
    b   is smelling
    c   not smelling

9   Give these signed copies _____ readers of our magazine.
    a   for
    b   to
    c   -

10 She entered the museum, _____ at an exhibit, and quickly ran out.
    a   looked at
    b   was looking
    c   did look

11 I _____ stay with my uncle during the summer.
    a   use to
    b   used
    c   would

12 The millionaire _____ having no money.
    a   wasn't used to
    b   didn't use to
    c   got used

Vocabulary

A Match.

 a
 b
 c
 d
 e
 f

1 performer b
2 pitch ☐
3 ticket ☐
4 spectator ☐
5 squad ☐
6 stand ☐

B Find six leisure-related words and use them to complete the sentences.

M	O	N	R	E	P	L	I	C	A	D	P
S	E	R	T	P	Y	E	L	A	F	O	A
E	U	P	O	R	T	R	A	I	N	E	R
N	M	R	T	Q	N	P	M	E	U	P	T
S	S	C	I	W	O	A	T	O	F	S	I
A	P	L	T	A	A	I	P	C	X	M	C
T	Q	O	W	T	B	O	B	T	M	V	I
I	R	A	N	S	T	S	A	W	U	C	P
O	Z	Z	R	V	O	N	C	A	C	I	A
N	P	F	I	E	K	G	I	R	B	U	N
S	S	P	E	C	T	A	C	L	E	O	T
S	U	P	P	O	R	T	E	R	O	M	Y

1 Adel has been an al-Ahly _____supporter_____ since he was a boy.

2 Our _____ is forever telling us to work harder.

3 There can't be only one _____ in the race!

4 The members of the group are young but they've already become _____ .

5 This _____ of a fighter plane is very realistic!

6 The young performers put on a great _____ .

C Complete the dialogue with these words.

breathtaking   keep   raise   remote   show off   ~~star~~

Journalist: Hey, Mr Chapman, can you tell us what you thought of the team's performance tonight?

Mr Chapman: Some players gave (1) _____star_____ performances, it just wasn't enough to win the match.

Journalist: This is the sixth time this season Grantham City has lost. What are you going to do about it?

Mr Chapman: I don't mean to (2) _____ but it's the first time we've had a bad season. Let's (3) _____ our fingers crossed that next week's match will have a better result.

Journalist: What about young sensation Barry Tailor? He managed to put some (4) _____ goals in the net at the beginning of the season, but hasn't scored since last month.

Mr Chapman: Remember players don't work by (5) _____ control. Sometimes they do well, sometimes they don't. I'm positive his performance will be much better soon.

Journalist: The owner of the team is giving £1000 to charity for every goal the team scores this year. How much do you think you'll (6) _____?

Mr Chapman: We'll just have to wait till the end of the season to find out!

Grammar

A Look at the pictures and write T (true) or F (false).

1 She's been painting for years. ☐ T
2 He hasn't caught anything. ☐
3 She hasn't fallen off the horse. ☐
4 She has been studying. ☐
5 His face has been painted. ☐
6 They have been running. ☐

B Circle the correct words.

1 'Why is your face red?' 'I have been jogging / jogged.'
2 How many games have we been winning / won so far?
3 They have played / been playing tennis since 10 am.
4 All participants have been given / giving a certificate.
5 The spectators have paid / been paying 50 pounds for the tickets.
6 The trainer has been hurting / hurt herself so there's no training today.

C Answer the questions about yourself.

1 What sports have you played this month?
_____

2 How long have you been a fan of your favourite sports team?
_____

3 What have you been doing for the past hour?
_____

4 How many leisure activities have you done this week?
_____

5 What activity have you taken up recently?
_____

6 Have you been watching any spectator sports these days? If so, which ones?
_____

Vocabulary

A Circle the odd one out.

1 rapids	gorge	⟨encounters⟩
2 risky	cautious	reckless
3 common	sheer	steep
4 river boarding	microlight plane	white water rafting
5 timid	bold	adventurous

B Circle the correct words.

Are you an adventurous person looking for an exciting way to spend your (1) spare / designated time? Then reach for the stars in a microlight plane!

Microlighting is a(n) (2) unique / amateurish experience. It (3) is / gets head and shoulders above most other leisure activities because it's exhilarating but it also allows you to slow down the (4) pace / drop a bit. Once you're in mid-air, you will have fantastic views of the surrounding countryside. It will definitely make a lasting (5) contact / impression on you.

Do you think it's too risky? Don't worry because your safety always comes first. All our trainers are extremely (6) professional / dull and don't take any unnecessary risks. They will also let you (7) in on / off with all the secrets of flying a microlight plane.

Sign up today! You won't be (8) taking it easy / let down!

For more information visit our website www.skysthelimit.co.uk or call 2389 33377.

C Match.

1 Please sit	a soaked on the rapids.
2 Don't let on	b fireworks off in the forest.
3 We always get	c to Dad we're going gorge swinging.
4 I'm scared! Let	d goes with the flow.
5 Don't let those	e me out of the boat!
6 He's very relaxed and always	f still on the canoe.

Grammar

A Complete the sentences with these words. Use each word once only.

> that   when   where   ~~which~~   who   whom   whose   why

1   Bungee jumping, _____which_____ is an extreme sport, is only for the bold.
2   That's the river _____ we went white water rafting.
3   Do you know the reason _____ the guide let the group down?
4   Jane, _____ is a karate expert, is my cousin.
5   To _____ do these hiking boots belong?
6   There was a time _____ old Mrs Neville was really adventurous.
7   This is the trail _____ I was telling you about.
8   I've no idea _____ microlight plane this is.

B Choose the correct answers.

1   There's a gorge near here _____ we can go hiking.
    (a) where
    b   that
    c   which

2   Moonbow gazing is something _____ I have never done.
    a   that
    b   who
    c   why

3   River boarding, _____ is done on the rapids, is exhilarating.
    a   that
    b   where
    c   which

4   That's the climber _____ leg is broken.
    a   who
    b   whom
    c   whose

5   1994 was the year _____ we first went ice skating.
    a   when
    b   which
    c   where

6   This is the sports centre in _____ you can do many activities.
    a   where
    b   which
    c   that

C Complete the paragraph with when, where or that.

Today is the day (1) _____that_____ we have been waiting for. We're all heading for the camp
(2) _____ our guide told us to meet her. Then we're going hiking in a tropical forest
(3) _____ some beautiful bright coloured birds live. We want to see if we can catch
a glimpse of some of them. It's a kind of bird (4) _____ you don't see very often and this
is our only chance to see it. I'm so excited. This isn't the first time we've been hiking together. 2006 was the
year (5) _____ we first went hiking as a group. We had such a fantastic time together that
we agreed to go hiking in a new place at least once every six months. Up until now, we have gone for walks
in areas close to the town (6) _____ we live. But now look where we are going – a tropical
forest! This is sure to be our biggest adventure yet.

Vocabulary

Complete the sentences with these words.

| adventurous | breathtaking | bungee | ~~ears~~ | keen | loose | miss |

1 I can't believe my _____ *ears* _____! It's £600 to go waterskiing!
2 The kids want to go camping but we're not _____ on it.
3 We're at a(n) _____ end tomorrow so let's go for coffee.
4 That new film sounds boring so I'm going to give it a(n) _____ .
5 We're going _____ jumping! Fantastic!
6 The view from the hill is absolutely _____ .
7 Henry doesn't like extreme sports. He isn't very _____ .

Listening

A 🎧 **Listen to the dialogue and change the words in bold to make the sentences true.**

1 The Ghana holiday offers **going on safari** as an activity.   *hiking*
2 The ten-day holiday to Ghana costs **£1,000** per person.   _____
3 Anton has always wanted to go to **Chile**.   _____
4 The water sports are for **children only**.   _____
5 The New Zealand holiday is for **three weeks**.   _____
6 Carmela agrees to let the others teach her to **bungee jump**.   _____

B 🎧 **Listen and tick (✓) the correct pictures.**

1 Where is the speaker?

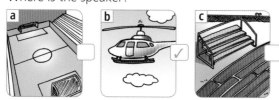

2 Which raffle ticket wins a book?

3 Which event is on at the moment?

4 Which objects are on the table?

5 What day is it today?

6 Which activity isn't available at the sports centre?

Speaking

A Look at these pictures and write 1 (picture 1) or 2 (picture 2) in each of the boxes.

1 I'm not sure, but maybe _____ .

  a she's a professional `2`

  b she's a beginner `1`

2 The woman is probably _____ .

  a about to fall

  b enjoying herself

3 I guess she is feeling really _____ .

  a scared

  b excited

4 It's possible that she _____ .

  a has been doing this for years

  b is having her first lesson

B Write three sentences for each of the pictures in A. Use the expressions from the *Remember!* box.

1 *It takes a lot of energy to go cycle racing.*

2 _____

3 _____

4 _____

5 _____

6 _____

C Work with a partner and take it in turns to describe what's happening in the pictures in A and say how you think the people are feeling. Student A should talk about picture 1 and student B should talk about picture 2.

Which leisure activities are best for someone your age who wants to

a keep fit?

b relax?

Vocabulary

Match.

1 Thanks for
2 Let me tell you about
3 The first activity is
4 Another activity
5 The highlight has been gazing
6 Speak to

a at the stars every night.
b is horse riding.
c the activities I've been doing.
d mountain climbing, isn't it?
e your last email.
f you soon.

Remember!

You should always edit a piece of writing when you have finished it. This means you have to review it and check for mistakes. Remember to look for errors with grammar, word order, punctuation, spelling and vocabulary.

Model writing task

Read the writing task and the model email and choose the correct answers.

I can't believe a new leisure centre has opened up near you. It must be great. What kind of activities are on offer there? Which ones would you recommend? Send me an email soon.

1	(a)	haven't written	b	not write	c	am not writing
2	a	too busy	b	busy enough	c	busy too
3	a	?	b	,	c	!
4	a	activites	b	activities	c	activity
5	a	year's	b	years	c	years'
6	a	concentrating	b	concentrated	c	concentration
7	a	brilliant	b	briliant	c	brillant
8	a	-	b	a	c	an

model composition

○○○   **Email**

New   Reply   Forward   Print   Delete   Send & Receive

Hi Nadia,

Thanks for your last email. Sorry I (1) _____ sooner. I've been (2) _____ to write emails lately because I've been going to the new leisure centre every day after school. It's fantastic there (3) _____

Let me tell you about some of the (4) _____ I've been doing. The first one is badminton. I play three times a week and I've already become quite good at it. The trainer says I'll be able to play in this (5) _____ local championships if I work hard enough. It takes a lot of skill and (6) _____ to play badminton so I'll have to try my best.

Another activity is aquarobics. I do this every Wednesday evening. It's a (7) _____ way to keep fit and you don't have to be able to swim to do it. You know how I was always too frightened to learn how to swim. Well, aquarobics has really helped me with my fear.

The best thing about the leisure centre is the youth club, however. It gives us (8) _____ opportunity to get together and organise activities that we're all really interested in. Let's go together the next time you're in town.

Speak to you soon,

Dalia

Grammar

A Circle the correct words.

1 It's (too) / enough cold outside to go jogging.
2 Are there too / enough tickets for all of us?
3 Is it hot enough / too to go swimming yet?
4 Not everybody is enough determined / determined enough to climb mountains.
5 There are too / enough many people in the canoe.
6 All the activities are cheap enough / too cheap for everyone to afford.

B Put the words in the correct order to make sentences.

1 clever / chess / not / to / play / enough / I'm
   I'm not clever enough to play chess.

2 club / members / too / to / the / accept / full / is / new
   _____

3 ? / scared / rafting / you / to / are / go / too
   _____

4 enough / extreme / for / exhilarating / enthusiasts / it's / sports
   _____

5 hike / takes / much / it / time / to / gorge / too / the / to
   _____

6 balls / everyone / there / for / enough / aren't
   _____

Your writing task

A Read the writing task and complete the plan for your email with the sentences and phrases in the box.

This is part of an email you received from an English-speaking friend.

> Your school sports day must have been a lot of fun. Which events did you take part in? Which one do you recommend? See you soon.

Now write an email answering your friend's questions.

a Briefly talk about the sports day in general.	Greeting: _____d_____
b Describe another event you took part in.	Paragraph 1: _____
c Describe one of the events you took part in.	Paragraph 2: _____
d Hi Sam,	Paragraph 3: _____
e Love, (your name)	Paragraph 4: _____
f Say which event you recommend and why.	Closing sentence: _____
g Speak to you soon.	Signing off: _____

B Now write your email.

Vocabulary

A Write R (Rural) or U (Urban).

1 picturesque   R
2 large scale
3 hustle and bustle

4 lack of facilities
5 bright lights
6 peace and quiet

B Complete the crossword puzzle.

Across

2 This region is full of apple and pear _____ .
5 I prefer _____ environments to the countryside.
6 For me, there aren't any _____ of living in a fishing village.
7 We're really _____ to be residents of the capital city.
8 The ins and _____ of making a roof garden will be explained later.

Down

1 The residents are fighting _____ and nail to save their houses.
3 There are pros and _____ to living in large cities.
4 There aren't _____ leisure facilities in our town; there's nothing for young people to do.

C Match.

1 There are too many
2 Clark wouldn't recommend life
3 All the necessary facilities are within walking
4 You live in very picturesque
5 Everything works well in
6 Life on a farm isn't all doom

a distance of our house.
b our district.
c in the sticks.
d and gloom.
e distractions in big cities.
f surroundings.

Grammar

A Complete the sentences with the correct form of the Past Perfect Continuous of the verbs in brackets.

1 We _____had been living_____ (live) in Cairo for two years before we moved to Marsa Matruh.
2 It _____ (rain) in the village, so the streets were wet.
3 _____ they _____ (water) the plants when the accident happened?
4 She _____ (not cycle) in the forest for long when she saw a squirrel.
5 I _____ (look) forward to seeing the bright lights of the city for months.
6 _____ he _____ (work) in our district when you first met?

B Look at the pictures, complete the questions and write short answers. Use the words given and the Past Perfect Continuous.

1

the sun / shine
Had the sun been shining
all year?
Yes, it had.

2

he / paint
_____
when you arrived?
_____

3

Brenda / wait / for long
_____
when Pete showed up?
_____

4

the woman / drinking juice
_____
at the café?
_____

5

it / snow
_____
for days on the mountain?
_____

6

they / sleep
_____
when you saw them
_____

C Complete the sentences with the Past Perfect Continuous of these verbs.

| build | not tour | plant | stand | ~~talk~~ | wait |

1 Pete _____had been talking_____ to the farmer for over an hour.
2 We _____ at the traffic lights when an ambulance rushed past.
3 They _____ the town for long when they met their cousin.
4 The company _____ skycrapers in the town centre when the owner died.
5 _____ the gardener _____ flowers at the time?
6 I _____ on a table when I slipped and fell.

33

Vocabulary

A Complete the word groups with these words.

~~adventure playground~~   bald eagle   community   species   suburb

1	botanical garden	public park	*adventure playground*
2	residential area	neighbourhood	
3	wildlife	creatures	
4	komodo dragon	polar bear	
5	residents	neighbours	

B Complete the poster with these words.

community centre   conservation   ~~destruction~~   natural habitat   policies   wild

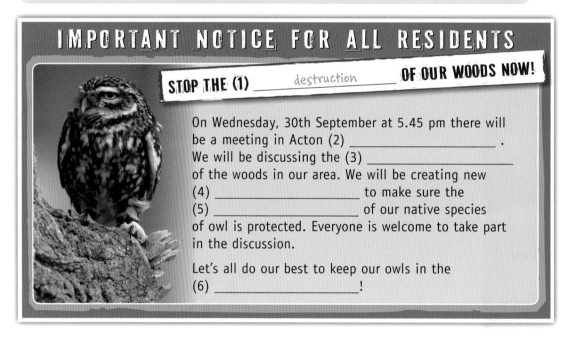

IMPORTANT NOTICE FOR ALL RESIDENTS

STOP THE (1) ___*destruction*___ OF OUR WOODS NOW!

On Wednesday, 30th September at 5.45 pm there will be a meeting in Acton (2) _____ .
We will be discussing the (3) _____ of the woods in our area. We will be creating new
(4) _____ to make sure the
(5) _____ of our native species of owl is protected. Everyone is welcome to take part in the discussion.

Let's all do our best to keep our owls in the
(6) _____!

C Circle the correct words.

1   Are komodo dragons (native) / far from home to this area?
2   There's nothing I enjoy more than cycling in captivity / open country.
3   How many animals gain / reside in this zoo?
4   We all have a role / condition to play in saving endangered species.
5   Our way of activity / life shouldn't harm other creatures.
6   The new park is a breath of fresh air / open space for the community.

Grammar

A Choose the correct answers.

1 They _____ the animals, so they got soaked.
   a washed
   b have washed
   c had been washing *(circled)*

2 This community _____ a lot since I was a child.
   a has changed
   b has been changing
   c was changed

3 The residents had _____ for a long time what the noise was.
   a wonder
   b been wondering
   c wondering

4 Polar bears _____ guests of this zoo for ten years.
   a have been
   b have been being
   c were being

5 We _____ the destruction of the natural habitat for decades before action was taken.
   a caused
   b had been causing
   c had caused

6 The bald eagles had _____ by the time we reached the area.
   a been migrating
   b been migrated
   c migrated

B Complete the sentences with the Past Perfect Simple or the Past Perfect Continuous of the verbs in brackets.

1 _____Had_____ the boy _____been looking_____ (look) at the seals when he fell into the water?

2 The adventure playground _____ (not built) by 2010.

3 Researchers _____ (study) the creature for months when it gave birth.

4 They _____ (walk) through mud, so they were very dirty.

5 _____ the zoo _____ (improve) since the last time you went there?

6 We _____ (not live) in the suburbs for long when I had to change job.

C Look at the pictures and write short answers to the questions.

Had all the lights gone out in the village?
No, they hadn't.

Had the dog been running when the photographer took the picture?
_____

Had he been riding the donkey home?
_____

Had the houses been painted different colours?
_____

Had the cars stopped to let the people cross the road?
_____

Had the tree been cut down?
_____

Vocabulary

Write the correct words.

bicycle lane   bright lights   country park   ~~inner city~~   public library   shopping mall

1 _____inner city_____   2 _____   3 _____

4 _____   5 _____   6 _____

Listening

A 🎧 Listen to April and Tony talking about things they have to do. Tick (✓) the correct boxes.

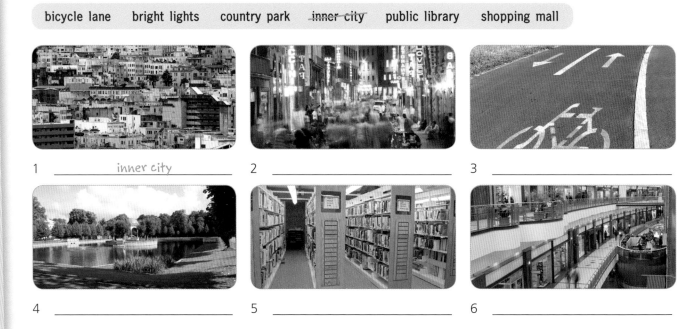

	April	Tony
1 edit talk on inner cities		✓
2 take leaflets to public library		
3 attend bicycle lanes opening		
4 speak to manager of shopping mall		
5 take kids to adventure playground		
6 organise trip to country park		

B 🎧 You will hear two teachers talking about students' suggestions on how to best use some land in a small town. Which use does each student suggest? For questions 1-5, write a letter (A-H) next to each name. There are three letters which you do not need to use.

1 Jade — H
2 Caroline — ☐
3 Jed — ☐
4 Michalis — ☐
5 Emma — ☐

A botanical garden
B residential area
C community centre
D zoo
E sports centre
F theatre
G adventure playground
H hospital

Speaking

A Complete the table about your perfect place to live. Put a tick (✓) or a cross (✗).

Remember!

When we are justifying our choices we use expressions like these.
More people would benefit from ...
... only appeals to young/old/sporty/etc people.
... would be more useful/better for the whole community.
... is more necessary/important than ...
... is missing in this city/town/village.
I think it's a good idea to ... because ...
There's a real need for ...
I don't see the point in + -ing .../... is pointless.
It's a waste of money to + infinitive .../... is a waste of money.

	It must have ...	I don't want ...	I don't mind if it has ...
cinema			
countryside			
emergency services			
good schools			
open space			
peace and quiet			
picturesque surroundings			
public parks			
restaurants			
sea			
shopping mall			
sports centre			

B Look at the task and pictures in C and complete these sentences based on your choices.

1 Living _____ only appeals to _____ .
2 _____ is more important to me than _____ .
3 I think it's a good idea to _____ because _____ .
4 I don't see the point in _____ .

C Look at the pictures below and talk to your partner about where you would like to live and where you would not like to live. Remember to justify your choices.

Discussion

'The peace and quiet of the countryside only appeals to old people.' Discuss.

Vocabulary

Circle the correct words.

1 I had never been in such a / so scary situation before.
2 It was the first hour / time I had ever been inside a cave.
3 The thunder storm was really terrified / scary.
4 The wind was howling and it was absolutely / immediately freezing.
5 At / In the end of the day, we all got home safely.
6 As fast / soon as we reached land, we jumped out of the boat.
7 I set the dog free without / then thinking.
8 All of a moment / sudden he started screaming.

 **Remember!**

When we are telling stories we use narrative tenses. The Past Simple, the Past Continuous, the Past Perfect Simple and the Past Perfect Continuous are the most common narrative tenses. Remember we normally only use present tenses if our story contains direct speech with speech marks.

Model writing task

Read the writing task and the model story below. Underline all examples of the Past Simple, Past Continuous, Past Perfect Simple and Past Perfect Continuous. How many examples are there of each tense?

Write a story which begins with this sentence:
We had all been looking forward to seeing the bright lights of the city.

model composition

London calling!

My family had all been looking forward to seeing the bright lights of the city. Olivia, Steven and I had been planning the trip to London for weeks and we were determined to have the time of our lives.

When we arrived at Euston Station we were all extremely excited. We had never been in such a huge train station before and we weren't used to all its hustle and bustle.

As soon as we got off the train, we headed for the London Eye. We had heard it was fantastic. Before long we were up in the sky looking at the entire city from above.

All of a sudden Steven started shaking badly. He had gone absolutely white and looked terrified. It was the first time he had been so high up. But there was nothing we could do. We had to wait until the wheel stopped to get off.

About an hour and three cups of strong tea later, Steven was feeling fine again. We continued our visit to the capital and at the end of the day we all agreed it had been one of the most interesting days of our lives.

Grammar

A Choose the correct answers.

1 We had decided to head for _____ River Seine.
  a the *(circled)*
  b a
  c -

2 Can you tell me where _____ nearest hospital is?
  a -
  b the
  c a

3 Let's go to a restaurant in town for _____ supper.
  a the
  b a
  c -

4 I didn't know your dad was from _____ Malta.
  a -
  b a
  c the

5 He's _____ man who works at the country practice.
  a a
  b -
  c the

6 There's _____ adventure playground near here.
  a an
  b the
  c a

B Underline and correct the errors in some of the sentences. Tick (✓) the correct sentences.

1 There are too many <u>the</u> distractions in big cities. _____ *many distractions* _____

2 This is a most beautiful bridge I've ever seen. _____

3 Lack of facilities is a drawback in most rural areas. _____

4 We're going to theatre this evening. _____

5 Is there hospital in this town? _____

6 What are we having for the lunch? _____

7 She wrote a shocking report on inner cities. _____

8 Let's stop here for the bite to eat. _____

Your writing task

A Read the writing task and complete the plan for your story with your own ideas based on the sentence given.

Write a story that begins with this sentence:
It was the most picturesque village I had ever been to.

Title: _____
Paragraph 1: _____
Paragraph 2: _____
Paragraph 3: _____
Paragraph 4: _____
Paragraph 5: _____

B Now write your story.

Reading

A Read the text about a special festival on Moab Mountain.

Look Mum! No hands!

Moab Mountain in Utah, USA, is a breathtaking place to visit. This is desert land and its cliffs and canyons are made of hard, red rock. It's the perfect destination for those who want a break from the hustle and bustle of the city, but who also want all the fun of an extreme location. Moab is a popular venue for mountain biking, half marathons and Jeep safari. In recent years, it has also become a unicycling playground.

Every year at the end of March, the International Moab Mountain Unicycle Festival takes place. The first festival, which was held in 2000, had only five participants. However, today the festival attracts around 200 participants as well as hundreds of spectators. Riders of all abilities turn up to show off their skills on these funny bikes with one wheel.

During the festival there are competitions for the riders. Beginners compete to see who can ride the longest using only one foot to pedal. Professional riders take more risks and take part in a competition where they jump down sheer drops in the rock. There's also a 'joker' competition in which participants compete to see who can ride the longest on a unicycle which doesn't have a seat. There are great prizes on offer. Even spectators are given the chance to win a prize by buying raffle tickets.

Moab doesn't just attract cyclists during the annual festival, however. Around 150,000 riders come here throughout the year to practise their favourite sport. Moab provides them with much more of a challenge than open country does. This makes it one of the world's most thrilling locations for riders. In fact, it has become so popular that there are now many campsites and hotels in the district to provide accommodation for extreme sports enthusiasts. If you're a cycling fan, then why not get on your bike and head for the mountains?

B Write A if the sentence is correct and B if it is not correct.

1 Moab Mountain is part of a desert. `A`

2 Bicycles are the only vehicles allowed on Moab Mountain. ☐

3 200 people participated in the first Unicycle Festival. ☐

4 Professional riders always use unicycles that they can't sit on. ☐

5 Moab attracts visitors all year round. ☐

6 Visitors don't have to stay in tents. ☐

Vocabulary

Choose the correct answers.

1 There are eleven players on the _____ .
   - (a) squad
   - b pitch
   - c scale

2 What are the pros and _____ of team sports?
   - a cons
   - b outs
   - c drawbacks

3 There are 150 species of tree in the _____ garden.
   - a replica
   - b botanical
   - c adventure

4 I don't know how this model plane _____ .
   - a resides
   - b performs
   - c works

5 The successful young volleyball player quickly became a _____ .
   - a sensation
   - b spectator
   - c stand

6 It was absolutely _____ to ride through open country.
   - a timid
   - b exhilarating
   - c privileged

7 They _____ a lot of money selling raffle tickets.
   - a raised
   - b supported
   - c inspired

8 You are very _____ not to do risky sports.
   - a wise
   - b dull
   - c delicate

9 What is life in the _____ like?
   - a surroundings
   - b sticks
   - c venue

10 The fans have stopped _____ the team.
    - a showing off
    - b letting off
    - c cheering on

11 Our guide seemed quite _____ at times.
    - a sufficient
    - b amateurish
    - c picturesque

12 What is the komodo dragon's natural _____ like?
    - a community
    - b habitat
    - c trail

Grammar

Choose the correct answers.

1 Let's gaze at _____ moon.
   - a -
   - b a
   - (c) the

2 Bungee jumping was _____ fantastic experience.
   - a an
   - b a
   - c the

3 I _____ my leg so I can't go hiking.
   - a have been breaking
   - b had broken
   - c have broken

4 It's _____ to go cycling. Let's stay in instead.
   - a too windy
   - b windy enough
   - c enough windy

5 1993 was the year in _____ the community centre opened.
   - a which
   - b when
   - c that

6 The player _____ round the pitch when the bottle hit him.
   - a had been running
   - b has been running
   - c had ran

7 The artist _____ me to take up painting.
   - a has been inspiring
   - b has inspired
   - c had been inspiring

8 Is that the trainer _____ gave you a lift home?
   - a that
   - b -
   - c whom

9 Springburn Park is _____ popular attraction.
   - a the
   - b a
   - c -

10 'Have you been waiting long?' 'No, _____ .'
    - a we hadn't
    - b we haven't
    - c you haven't

11 The inner city isn't _____ for me to live in.
    - a enough picturesque
    - b too picturesque
    - c picturesque enough

12 This is the park _____ we first met.
    - a when
    - b where
    - c which

Vocabulary

A Write the missing letters.

1 Something extremely clever is this.   i <u>n g e n i o u s</u>
2 This is a person who writes about places he or she has visited.   t _ _ _ _ _   w _ _ _ _ _
3 We use this phrase to refer to detailed information.   f _ _ _ _ _ a _ _ f _ _ _ _ _ _
4 This is a journey to learn new things.   v _ _ _ _ _ o _ d _ _ _ _ _ _ _ _ _
5 This is printed material like a book or a magazine.   p _ _ _ _ _ _ _ _ _ _
6 These are where you come from.   r _ _ _ _

B Complete the sentences with these words.

> broaden   ~~enable~~   ensure   shorten   trace   update

1 This travel pass will _____*enable*_____ you to travel all over the city.
2 The travel agency will _____ its website soon to include new destinations.
3 Rebecca wants to _____ the journey her ancestors made.
4 Please _____ your seatbelt is fastened for landing.
5 Will space travel really _____ our horizons?
6 We're going to have to _____ our trip to the Grand Canyon if we want to catch the train.

C Circle the correct words.

1 What is your (current) / interactive location?
2 Lee is of Chinese reconstruction / descent.
3 In some countries it's impossible to enlighten / enforce a no-smoking ban.
4 The sponsored walk is in aid of a(n) worthy / award-winning cause.
5 Turn to page 39 in your atlases / globes.
6 Travelling to other continents will sharpen / enrich your lives.

Grammar

A Look at the pictures and write T (true) or F (false).

1   The plane is going to land.   `F`
2   Joe will be sleeping soon.   ☐
3   Phillipa's journey to London will take a long time tomorrow.   ☐
4   The horse isn't going to jump over the fence.   ☐
5   They're going to fall into the river.   ☐
6   The family won't be late for the ferry.   ☐

B Complete the TV announcement with the correct form of the Future Simple, be going to or the Future Continuous of the verbs in brackets. Sometimes more than one answer is possible.

Tonight G-TV (1) _____will enable_____ (enable) its viewers to travel to remote corners of the globe. From 7.30 to 9.00 Emma Martin (2) _____ (take) us on the journey of a lifetime to the Seychelles. She (3) _____ (tell) us everything we need to know about the various kinds of holidays on offer on these spectacular islands. If you (4) _____ (travel) to the Seychelles soon, don't miss it. After that Lou Brahma (5) _____ (present) reconstructions of holiday disasters in *Wish You Weren't Here?*. I'm sure the programme (6) _____ (give) useful advice to first-time travellers abroad. And finally at 10.15 viewers (7) _____ (have) the chance to share their own stories of interesting journeys they have made in *Viewers' Voyages*. The programme only started last week, but it looks like it (8) _____ (be) a huge success.

C Answer the questions.

1   Where will you be going for your next holiday?

_____

2   How will you get to school on Monday?

_____

3   When are you going to learn to drive?

_____

4   You have won a trip to the USA. Which cities will you visit?

_____

5   Where will you go swimming in the summer?

_____

6   Will you be travelling this time next week?

_____

43

Vocabulary

A Match.

1 The explorers set   a Antarctica's sub-zero temperatures?
2 How can you tolerate   b on track.
3 Always look at the map to keep   c the assistance of a GPS?
4 A huge ice floe   d all odds.
5 We made it back home against   e themselves tough goals.
6 Did the travellers have   f was drifting in the icy waters.

B Complete the paragraph with these words.

| battle | capabilities | endure | exploits | lead | limits | set off | struggle |

Many people love travelling to remote locations in dangerous conditions. Not all of them have good experiences, though. In 1998, Italian skier and climber Marco Giannini really tested himself to the (1) _____*limits*_____ . It was February and he decided to (2) _____ for the snowy mountains of the Alps on his own. Marco was the kind of person who couldn't understand people who (3) _____ sedentary lives. His (4) _____ and adventures were well known and his friends were always amazed by his skills and (5) _____ . Whenever he came across difficulties while climbing, he would always (6) _____ on until he succeeded in reaching his goal. He even claimed that he could (7) _____ anything. That February turned out to be his last adventure, however. He fell and broke his leg and he had to (8) _____ to survive. He lay helpless for a day in the snow until the rescue services got to him. After that Marco decided to give up his life of adventure.

C Find six words related to exploring limits and complete the sentences.

A	C	S	U	M	P	L	I	S	M	O	D
C	R	A	N	T	D	I	F	M	A	S	E
C	G	P	W	D	N	M	L	O	Y	P	T
O	S	Y	F	L	O	A	T	I	N	G	E
M	I	M	A	K	C	T	Q	F	L	N	R
P	X	I	L	S	T	A	B	L	E	V	M
L	I	L	P	D	V	T	A	O	P	K	I
I	J	I	M	Z	P	I	V	A	O	N	N
S	Y	T	H	U	G	P	L	E	Y	P	A
H	H	T	F	A	B	N	N	I	O	L	T
M	I	E	P	R	N	S	U	N	R	G	I
E	X	S	N	Y	E	L	V	G	W	M	O
N	D	E	S	T	O	R	T	U	R	E	N
T	L	I	M	I	T	A	T	I	O	N	S

1 Climbing Mount Everest is an amazing _____*accomplishment*_____ .
2 It was sheer _____ that made us continue through the rainforest.
3 Watch out! That bridge isn't _____ .
4 The explorers grabbed onto a(n) _____ branch.
5 Why do people _____ themselves by going on dangerous expeditions?
6 I know my _____ and don't take too many risks.

Grammar

A Write questions and short answers with the Future Perfect Simple.

1 the expedition / end / by Friday ✓
  Will the expedition have ended by Friday?
  Yes, it will.

2 we / accomplish great things / this time next year ✓
  _____
  _____

3 they / publish the atlas / before January ✗
  _____
  _____

4 she / test herself to the limits / on the journey ✗
  _____
  _____

5 I / settle in at the hotel / by Wednesday ✓
  _____
  _____

6 you and Tom / reach the North Pole / by spring ✗
  _____
  _____

7 John / struggle in difficult conditions ✗
  _____
  _____

8 the GPS / assist the travellers ✓
  _____
  _____

B Complete the sentences with the Future Perfect Continuous of these verbs.

not ride	sell	struggle
talk	tour	wait

1 She _____will have been waiting_____ for the train for an hour soon.

2 The company _____ the atlas for a decade by March.

3 _____ we _____ Europe for two months tomorrow?

4 They _____ against the waves for hours.

5 Colin _____ a horse for the whole day.

6 _____ Carla _____ to the tourists for hours by the time we get there?

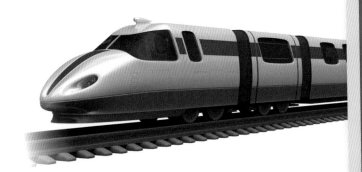

C Circle the correct answers.

1 We _____ this worthy cause for five years on Tuesday.
  a will support
  b will have been supporting ⃝
  c have supported

2 The GPS will _____ them on track during their voyage.
  a have kept
  b been keeping
  c kept

3 How many countries _____ by next month?
  a she will have visited
  b will she have visited
  c she has visited

4 'Will you have been travelling all day?'
  'No, _____ .'
  a I haven't
  b I won't have been
  c I won't

5 Gordon will have reached the river _____ .
  a before
  b yet
  c by now

6 Cathy will have been climbing in the Pyrenees _____ tomorrow.
  a for a week
  b by next week
  c this time next week

45

Vocabulary

Write the correct words.

camper van   catamaran   double-decker bus
glider   jet ski   moped

jet ski

Listening

A 🎧 Listen to three people talking about travelling. Tick (✓) the reasons why they choose to travel as they do.

	Anita (moped)	Randy (bus)	David (walking)
not time consuming			
keeps you fit			
inexpensive			
convenient		✓	
environmentally friendly			

B 🎧 You will hear a radio interview. For each question, put a tick (✓) in the correct box.

1 Gerald now misses his
   a family and friends. ☐
   b adventures. ✓
   c own bed. ☐

2 To travel the world, it took Gerald
   a less than eighty days. ☐
   b almost two years. ☐
   c more than three years. ☐

3 Gerald is currently
   a making Christmas presents. ☐
   b working in a bookshop. ☐
   c writing a book. ☐

4 *Against All Odds* will be in the shops in
   a August. ☐
   b September. ☐
   c November. ☐

5 *Against All Odds* is
   a a collection of short stories. ☐
   b a list of bus and train timetables. ☐
   c a complete travel guide. ☐

6 Gerald used his camper van
   a to get to Tasmania. ☐
   b for most of her trip. ☐
   c to tour small islands. ☐

Speaking

A For each question, place a tick (✓) in one of the columns to show your opinion.

	I agree	I agree to a certain extent	I disagree
Skiing is too dangerous.			
Activity holidays are thrilling.			
Travelling by train is exhausting.			
You don't get to see many places when you fly.			
Water sports keep you fit.			
Travelling from country to country is too time consuming.			

Remember!

When we are balancing arguments we use expressions like these.

On the one hand, people choose this kind of travel/go on this kind of holiday because ...

In addition, this kind of holiday/journey/trip is popular with people who ...

Another benefit/advantage of this kind of holiday/journey/trip is ...

Commuters/Holidaymakers/Backpackers are also able to/can also ...

On the other hand,/However, going on this kind of holiday/journey/trip means ...

Another disadvantage/drawback is ...

B Look at the advert in C and write sentences about the trip using the expressions from the *Remember!* box and these words.

convenient environmentally friendly exhausting impractical ~~inexpensive~~

1   On the one hand, people choose to travel by train because it's inexpensive.

2   _____

3   _____

4   _____

5   _____

C You and your partner have decided to go travelling together for a month this summer. Read the advert for a trip and discuss its advantages and disadvantages with your partner. Then decide together if you will take the trip. Remember to justify your choices.

France   Spain   Switzerland   Holland

Explore your limits!

Are you looking for the adventure of a lifetime? Then join us on our European activity tour this summer!

★ 3-star accommodation and all meals provided   ★ Total cost per person £1,800

Schedule

2nd June	Ferry from Dover to Calais; train from Calais to Paris
2nd – 5th June	Three days in beautiful Paris. Visit the Eiffel Tower, the Louvre, the Left Bank and much more!
5th June	Overnight train from Paris to Barcelona
6th – 13th June	One whole week in Barcelona and surroundings! Go jet skiing and fly a glider!
13th June	Overnight train from Barcelona to Tuscany
14th – 20th June	Tour the most picturesque countryside in Italy by moped.
21st – 22nd June	Flight from Tuscany to Geneva; coach to the Alps
22nd – 25th June	Three fun-filled days in the Swiss Alps!
26th June	Flight from Geneva to Amsterdam
26th – 30th June	Four nights in beautiful Amsterdam.

Discussion

'There are more advantages to travelling by plane than there are disadvantages.' Discuss.

Vocabulary

Match.

1	I was wondering	a	come touring with us this summer?
2	Would you like	b	the end of October?
3	Why don't you	c	to come for a ride on my moped?
4	Are you available at	d	be free next week.
5	I really hope	e	if you would like to come fishing with me.
6	Let me know if you'll	f	you'll be able to come with us.

Remember!

You can make informal writing more appealing by using strong adjectives. Try to use strong adjectives in all writing tasks, but remember not to use them too much as this can make your writing seem over-exaggerated.

Model writing task

Read the writing task and the model email and circle the strong adjectives.

Write an email inviting an English-speaking friend of yours to go backpacking.

model composition

⬤ ⬤ ⬤			Email		
📝 New	📩 Reply	📧 Forward	🖨 Print	🗑 Delete	📨 Send & Receive

Hi Annette,

How are you? I was speaking to Kelly last night and we had (1) a nice / an ingenious idea to go backpacking in Europe this summer. Why don't you come with us? Are you free in August?

We're going for four weeks and we'll be visiting some of the (2) most picturesque / nicest places in Europe. We'll be mainly travelling by train and ferry. It'll be (3) exhausting / tiring but that way we'll be able to see much more of the continent.

We're planning to go camping while we're away. Kelly says she's got a (4) big / massive tent that's big enough for the three of us. It'll be great as we'll be able to get close to nature. Another benefit is that it's (5) inexpensive / cheap accommodation so we'll be able to stay away longer than we would if we stayed in hotels. Also, you don't get to sleep under the stars in a hotel!

We'll both be really (6) glad / delighted if you come with us. We estimate that the total cost of the trip will be around £800. This should be sufficient to cover our tickets, food and spending money. Let me know if you'll be coming with us and we can all decide on our schedule together.

Speak soon,

Gayle

Grammar

A Choose the correct answers.

1 What time _____ from Munich on Saturdays?
   a is the bus arriving
   b will the bus have arrived
   c⃝ does the bus arrive

2 Careful! You _____ your ticket.
   a lose
   b are going to lose
   c will have lost

3 The cruise _____ in Hawaii.
   a is beginning
   b will be beginning
   c begins

4 The eagles _____ by now.
   a won't migrate
   b aren't migrating
   c won't have migrated

5 The journey _____ over soon.
   a will be
   b is
   c will have been

6 Jack really hopes they _____ him to go to Portugal this year.
   a will ask
   b will be asking
   c are asking

B Complete the sentences with these words.

> does   ~~going to~~   is   will   will have   will have been

1 The driver is _____ going to _____ faint!
2 Collette _____ studying migration for two years tomorrow.
3 When _____ Steve coming back from Ibiza?
4 _____ you ring the travel agent later?
5 When _____ the next bus to Chelsea leave?
6 They _____ booked the catamaran by the time we get back.

Your writing task

A Read the writing task and complete the plan with the words in the box.

Write an email inviting an English-speaking friend of yours to go on a cruise.

> ~~Dear~~   Give details about the cruise   Restate the invitation   Speak soon,
> Talk about one aspect   Tell your friend your plans

Greeting: _____ Dear _____ (friend's name),
Paragraph 1:   _____ and invite him / her to join you.
Paragraph 2:   _____ and the places you intend to visit.
Paragraph 3:   _____ of the cruise that will be appealing.
Paragraph 4   _____ and tell your friend how you can make arrangements.
Closing sentence: _____
Signing off: (Your name)

B Now write your email.

Vocabulary

A Write **H** (Housework), **P** (Physical leisure activity) or **S** (Sedentary activity).

1 rope climbing   P
2 washing the dishes ☐
3 tidying your room ☐
4 martial arts ☐

5 watching TV ☐
6 listening to music ☐
7 sweeping the floor ☐
8 aerobics ☐

B Complete the sentences with these words.

> balance category check-up escalator form peak root ~~weight~~

1 Eating sensibly helps you control your _____ *weight* _____ .
2 Laura's having a(n) _____ at the dentist's this evening.
3 Which _____ does housework come in?
4 The athlete hasn't been at his _____ for months now.
5 Shall we use the _____ or the stairs?
6 It can be difficult to get the _____ right between exercise and relaxation.
7 Hugh has finally got to the _____ of his health problem.
8 How do you manage to stay on _____?

C Complete the crossword puzzle.

Across

3 Aerobics _____ up a lot of calories.
6 You must _____ down on fatty foods.
7 Rope climbing helps you to _____ your muscles.
8 Have you _____ up for the martial arts class?

Down

1 Ballet dancers are incredibly _____ .
2 Don't be so _____! Take up a physical activity.
4 The heart _____ oxygen round the body.
5 How do you _____ your physical fitness?

Crossword grid:
1 Down: F L E X I B L E
2 Down: I
3 Across: B
4 Down: P
5 Down: M
6 Across: C
7 Across: S ... E
8 Across: S

50

Grammar

A Look at the pictures and write **T** (true) or **F** (false).

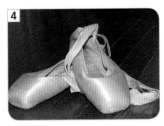  

1 Grandad can still do push-ups. ☐ T
2 Bill and Ben don't have to improve their diet. ☐
3 The children mustn't play football in the park. ☐
4 These can't be the dancer's shoes. ☐
5 Julia needn't be more active than she is already. ☐
6 He has to strengthen his muscles. ☐

B Circle the correct words.

1 You (can't) / don't have to go to the gym until you've finished the housework!
2 Would / Must you help me climb up the rope, please?
3 Yesterday they could / were able to eat ice cream at 4 o'clock.
4 'Need / Can I lose weight?' 'No, you don't have to. You're fine.'
5 She will can / be able to stay in shape by doing yoga.
6 Could / Would we go to the adventure playground please, Dad?

C Complete the paragraph with these words.

> are able   can   can't   don't have to   ~~have~~   must

We all (1) _____have_____ to look after ourselves. Our health depends on
how much exercise we do and how healthy the food we eat is. However, some people don't
have a problem with their weight, but they never exercise and their diets contain lots of fatty
and sugary foods. They sometimes ask, 'Why (2) _____ I go to the gym and eat
fruit and vegetables that I don't like when I'm already thin?' But just because you are thin doesn't mean
you (3) _____ watch what you eat or take physical exercise. Physical activity and
eating properly (4) _____ help us stay fit and healthy and that means we
(5) _____ to fight illnesses better. Don't worry, though, if you feel you
(6) _____ stop eating your favourite unhealthy snacks. You will make a big
difference to your health just by cutting down on them and doing a few extra everyday activities.

Vocabulary

A **Match.**

1 dairy   a information
2 packets of   b meal
3 ready   c habits
4 food   d labelling
5 nutritional   e product
6 eating   f food

B **Circle the correct words.**

1 A healthy nutrition / diet is the secret of staying in shape.
2 The talk will deal with the issue / obligation of diet.
3 Do you think you're allergic / intolerant of gluten?
4 Unfortunately the twins are prone to / from illness.
5 I didn't realise you suffer / prevent from allergies.
6 Do you take supplements / substances?

C **Complete the sentences with these words.**

apply   avoid   consume   function   indicate   label

1 What does a red light _____ indicate _____?
2 If you want to eat healthily, you should _____ foods with a lot of fat in them.
3 Does this advice _____ to everyone?
4 You shouldn't _____ so many sweets.
5 Some people can't _____ without coffee in the morning.
6 By law, food manufacturers must _____ their produce.

Grammar

A Match.

1. Ryan might go on a diet next week.
2. You ought to try making your own meals.
3. The new labelling system should be ready by next month.
4. May I try one of your plums?
5. They may not have another cake.
6. He may consume as much fruit as he likes.

a. Giving advice
b. Asking for permission
c. Giving permission
d. Refusing permission
e. Possibility
f. Prediction

B Write questions and short answers using the words given.

1. I / should / cut down on salt ✓
   Should I cut down on salt?
   Yes, you should.

2. Martin / should / do a first aid course ✓

3. they / may / come for dinner ✗

4. we / should / look after our personal hygiene ✓

5. she / may / consume dairy products ✗

6. the manufacturers / should / stop labelling food ✗

C Circle the sentence, a or b, that means the same as the first sentence.

1. He might take a job in a health food store.
   a. It's possible that he'll begin working in a health food store.
   b. We will allow him to go to work in a health food store.

2. They ought not to take those supplements.
   a. It's a bad idea for them to take those supplements.
   b. I refuse to give them permission to take those supplements.

3. May I eat this apple?
   a. Is it a good idea for me to eat this apple?
   b. Will you let me eat this apple?

4. The ready meal should be warm soon.
   a. My advice is to warm the ready meal soon.
   b. I predict the ready meal will be warm soon.

5. You may not have more nuts.
   a. I refuse to let you eat more nuts.
   b. It's impossible for you to eat more nuts.

6. Should we call the doctor?
   a. Do you advise us to call the doctor?
   b. Is it likely we'll call the doctor?

6 Lesson 3

Vocabulary

Circle the odd one out.

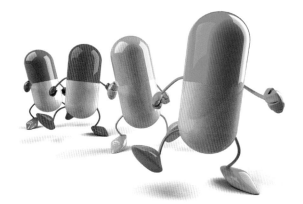

1 (gluten)   vitamin pills   supplements
2 nuts   ready meal   personal hygiene
3 yoga   martial arts   nutritional information
4 pain   ache   calorie
5 consume   digest   supplement

Listening

A 🎧 **You will hear six people talking about health and fitness. Circle the correct words.**

1 Nutrition / (Yoga) / Personal hygiene isn't a special feature of this month's issue.
2 The doctor said the speaker must not lose more weight / burn more calories / eat any fat.
3 The martial arts class is on at the same time as the first aid class / food supplements documentary / talk on yoga.
4 Clare becomes ill when she eats food which contains eggs / nuts / gluten.
5 The dessert mentioned is colour-coded with a green / amber / red light.
6 The speaker first got aches and pains on Tuesday / Wednesday / Thursday.

B 🎧 **Listen to a woman talking about food supplements and complete the notes.**

1 Sharin is an expert on _____ nutrition _____ .
2 Vitamin C is one of the most _____ people take today.
3 Vitamin C is important for our _____ and well-being.
4 Some pills contain as much vitamin C as _____ oranges.
5 Vitamin A is necessary for healthy eyes and _____ .
6 Too much vitamin A can cause _____ health problems.

Speaking

A Complete the dialogues with words from the *Remember!* box.

1 'Calum should see a doctor.'
'I couldn't _____ agree more _____ .'

2 'I've started taking vitamin pills.'
'I'm not sure _____ .'

3 'She needs to take care of her personal hygiene.'
'_____ you mean.'

4 'They should label their packaging better.'
'_____ I think.'

5 'The children must go on a diet.'
'_____ I don't agree.'

6 'Let's join the aerobics class.'
'_____ if we joined the yoga class.'

Remember!

When we are agreeing we use expressions like these.
Yes, I totally/completely/entirely agree with you.
I think you're right./You're absolutely right about ...
That's exactly what I think.
I see what you mean.
I couldn't agree more.

When we are disagreeing we use expressions like these.
I'm not sure that's a good idea.
I don't think that's the best option.
I'm afraid I don't agree.
I think it'd be better if/to ...

When we are conceding a point we use expressions like these.
You've got a point, but ...
I see what you're saying, but ...
I agree to a certain extent, but ...

B Look at the pictures in C and note one advantage and one disadvantage of each activity.

	1	2	3	4	5
Advantages					
Disadvantages					

C A friend of yours wants to improve his fitness and lose some weight. Look at the pictures of activities he's considering and talk to your partner about which ones you recommend he should take up and which ones you think he shouldn't take up.

Discussion

'Everyone should take food supplements'. Discuss.

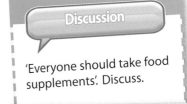

Vocabulary

Circle the correct words.

1   What / Why don't you try watching less TV?
2   One belief / idea would be to cut down on snacks.
3   Think about the long-term benefits / goods of regular physical exercise.
4   You could always / ever take up tennis if you don't like team sports.
5   Garlic is extremely good for / to you.

Remember!

In order to capture and keep readers' interest when writing articles, you should include special language features like directly addressing the reader, asking rhetorical questions for effect and using imperatives. These features make your writing more interesting.

Model writing task

Read the writing task and the model article and decide which language features (direct address, rhetorical questions or imperatives) appear in the highlighted sentences.

Write an article for your school magazine explaining why young people must look after their personal hygiene.

model composition

Who is the fairest of them all?

direct address   *rhetorical question*

Are you one of those people who just can't be bothered to look after your physical appearance? Does your personal hygiene not concern you very much? Then read on.

So, you're a young adult. You've got lots of demands on you. There just doesn't seem to be enough hours in the day sometimes for schoolwork and looking after yourself. Do you often say 'I should have worn my other T-shirt today' or 'Why couldn't I have taken time to wash my hair this morning!'? Then take action. It's very important to look after your appearance. Young people often feel embarrassed if their hair isn't looking good or if the clothes that they only bought a month ago are suddenly too small for them.

The good news is it can be easy to get back confidence in the way you look. One idea would be to talk about how you feel with your friends. Being honest about your feelings is very beneficial because it can help you see that most people are experiencing the same thing.

Why don't you give it a try? The next time you're not happy with your appearance, call up your closest friends and ask them for advice.

Grammar

Choose the correct answers.

1 You might have _____ us you were at the gym.
   a   tell
   b   to tell
   (c) told

2 I should _____ a kilo of ice cream.
   a   not have eaten
   b   have not eaten
   c   not eaten

3 It _____ have been Miles who scored the goal.
  He can't play football.
   a   must
   b   can't
   c   may not

4 Sarah could have joined the yoga class,
  but she _____ .
   a   did
   b   didn't
   c   couldn't

5 Those new tennis rackets _____ been very expensive.
   a   ought to have
   b   must have
   c   should have

6 The baby _____ have had an ear infection because
  he was pulling his ears.
   a   should
   b   can't
   c   may

Your writing task

A Read the writing task and complete the plan with ideas for your article.

Write an article for your school magazine giving advice to young people who pay too much attention to their appearance.

Title: _____

Paragraph 1:   Introduce issue to be discussed and make some general comments on it.

Paragraph 2:   Analyse nature of the problem.
                 (problem _____,
                 cause _____,
                 result _____)

Paragraph 3:   Provide specific advice on how to deal with the problem.
                 (advice: _____ and
                 _____)

Paragraph 4:   Sum up and give general advice about the issue.

B Now write your article.

Review 3

Reading

A Read the text about yoga.

Try this at home!

Are you looking for a new pastime that will create a balance between physical activity and relaxation? Then yoga may be the perfect choice for you. Yoga can be practised by people of all ages and levels of fitness. (1) __e__ It's a great way to strengthen your muscles and become more flexible.

In the 1930s, Indians Sri Tirumali Krishnamcharya and K Pattabhi Jois developed one of the most popular forms of yoga practised worldwide today. They worked together using an ancient Sanskrit text called Yoga Korunta to create a set routine of yoga movements and breathing exercises. (2) _____

Ashtanga is different from other forms of yoga. It is a very powerful form of aerobic exercise which creates deep heat in the body. (3) _____ In other forms of yoga, however, the routine can change each time and the stretching exercises aren't aerobic.

(4) _____ As well as making you stronger and more flexible, it can also help you to stay calm. By focusing on your breathing while doing physical exercise, you are able to get a balance between mind and body. In addition, yoga helps to make us healthier so we are less likely to get common illnesses like colds.

Furthermore, yoga encourages you to think about what you're doing. Often you will close your eyes while doing certain movements. (5) _____ After a few lessons you'll stop looking at what the others around you are doing. You will stop comparing yourself and start focusing on yourself.

If you're interested in yoga, but can't find a class near you, then it might be an excuse to travel. (6) _____ This could prove to be an ingenious way of getting to know new people, discovering beautiful new locations and staying in shape.

B Complete the text with these sentences.

a   The result of their co-operation was ashtanga yoga.

b   This allows you to concentrate better and it makes you less competitive.

c   Whatever kind of yoga you choose, there are many long-term benefits.

d   Recently, it has become extremely common for beginners as well as advanced yoga students to go on yoga holidays.

e   It can also be done anywhere at any time.

f   Every time someone practises ashtanga, he or she does exactly the same movements.

Vocabulary

Choose the correct answers.

1 Milk and cheese are _____ .
  a supplements
  b dairy products ⓑ
  c foundations

2 This book on nutrition will _____ you.
  a enlighten
  b nourish
  c strengthen

3 Mark is always _____ himself to the limits.
  a setting
  b testing
  c leading

4 Rachel has travelled all over the _____ .
  a globe
  b horizon
  c atlas

5 Shall we sign _____ for the safari?
  a on
  b down
  c up

6 The _____ fitness DVD was amazing.
  a interactive
  b flexible
  c intolerant

7 Clark is _____ to headaches.
  a ingenious
  b prone
  c allergic

8 I hate sailing, so I don't want to go in a _____ .
  a helicopter
  b rocket
  c dinghy

9 They _____ very high temperatures.
  a skipped
  b endured
  c pumped

10 Let's sit down to _____ our food.
  a enforce
  b digest
  c tolerate

11 Always read the _____ information on food labels.
  a environmentally friendly
  b impractical
  c nutritional

12 We all need to set ourselves _____ .
  a goals
  b roots
  c peaks

Grammar

Choose the correct answers.

1 _____ I go on holiday with Sam this summer, Mum?
  a Would
  b Ought
  c Could ⓒ

2 The rocket _____ through space this time tomorrow.
  a will be flying
  b is going to fly
  c flies

3 You _____ to have bought a ready meal.
  a mustn't
  b ought not
  c shouldn't

4 We _____ to take tents with us as the campsite has them.
  a can't
  b aren't able
  c don't have

5 The bus _____ be here any minute.
  a should
  b should have
  c must

6 Oh no, they _____ shorten our trip by three days.
  a will have
  b will be
  c are going to

7 We _____ late for the gym if we jog there.
  a won't have been
  b won't be
  c aren't

8 '_____ I bring a packed lunch?' 'No, you don't.'
  a Need
  b Should
  c Might

9 She _____ from the illness in time for the wedding.
  a will have been recovering
  b is recovering
  c will have recovered

10 Jamie _____ go to the match yesterday.
  a could
  b might have
  c was able to

11 You _____ have told us you were going skiing on your own!
  a must
  b should
  c may

12 Don't forget! Training _____ at 6.30.
  a begins
  b is beginning
  c will have begun

Vocabulary

A Match.

1 emission ☐ *e*
2 research ☐
3 population ☐
4 excellence ☐
5 extinction ☐

B Complete the advertisement with these words.

brush up   high flyer   refresh   research   scratch   ~~strong point~~

Are environmental issues not your (1) _____strong point_____ but you must pass a test on global warming this month? Don't worry, get up to (2) _____ with *Planet Master*!

Planet Master is an interactive DVD with all the latest information about the condition our planet is in today. It's ideal for students who want to (3) _____ their knowledge of the environment or who need to (4) _____ their memories in a fun, but effective way.

You can (5) _____ all the areas you have particular problems with. Surprise yourself and your teacher by becoming a (6) _____ in only a few weeks!

Planet Master is available for £65 plus postage. Order your copy today!

C Circle the correct words.

1 Let's keep our fingers crossed that the blue whale doesn't become emitted / extinct

2 Check / Find out this new atlas! It's fantastic.

3 Some people will stop / predict at nothing to help the environment.

4 The report on India is very well excellent / researched.

5 He's been travelling for years so he knows / emits his way around the globe.

6 This documentary will help you improve / excel your awareness of environmental pollution.

Grammar

A **Choose the correct answers.**

1 Rainbows _____ when the sun comes out after rain.
   a   are appearing
   ⓑ   appear
   c   appeared

2 If you do well in your geography test,
   I _____ you on a trip.
   a   will take
   b   would take
   c   take

3 _____ they do more research, they won't find
   ways to save the planet.
   a   If
   b   Unless
   c   When

4 If you _____ to be a high flyer, this DVD will help you.
   a   would want
   b   will want
   c   want

5 When the moon is bright, the stars _____
   usually visible.
   a   won't be
   b   aren't
   c   weren't

6 If I were you, I _____ the green group.
   a   would join
   b   will join
   c   joined

B **Match.**

1 If the sun is hot,   a   the planet would be in better shape.
2 Unless you brush up your knowledge of the globe,   b   the planet suffers.
3 Will you lend me your umbrella   c   will there be less pollution?
4 If we waste less energy,   d   if it rains?
5 When people stop caring,   e   do you stay in the shade?
6 If we saved the rainforests,   f   you won't pass the test.

C **Complete the sentences using zero, first or second conditionals.**

1 If I were in an environmental group, _____ .
2 When it snows, _____ .
3 Unless we take action soon, _____ .
4 If I had enough time and money, _____ .
5 If we recycle paper, glass and plastic, _____ .
6 If the temperature goes above forty degrees, _____ .

Vocabulary

A **Write the missing letters.**

1 You do this when you lose hope.   d _e_ _s_ _p_ _a_ _i_ _r_

2 This is another word for *disastrous*.   c _ _ _ _ _ _ _ _ _ _ _

3 This is when you place something with one side higher than the other.   t _ _ _

4 This is a network.   g _ _ _

5 This is the process of changing something from one form to another.   c _ _ _ _ _ _ _ _ _

6 This is a place where old products are processed to make new ones.   r _ _ _ _ _ _ _ _ _ p _ _ _ _

B **Look at the pictures and write FF (Fossil fuel) or RS (Renewable source) to show what they are examples of.**

C **Choose the correct answers.**

1 When do experts predict fossil fuels will _____?
   a run out
   b turn to
   c carry out

2 The farmers' market used to _____ place on a Saturday.
   a bring
   b take
   c carry

3 Let's join the buyers' _____ .
   a alternative
   b source
   c cooperative

4 How much electricity does your solar panel _____?
   a generate
   b bring about
   c convert

5 I'm sure using renewable energy sources will catch _____ .
   a up
   b out
   c on

6 The environmental group is against nuclear _____ .
   a warming
   b power
   c sunlight

Grammar

A Write sentences using the third conditional.

1 if / we / turn to / solar power / we / save money

   If we had turned to solar power, we would have saved money.

2 if only / people / not use / fossil fuels / our cities / cleaner

   _____

3 if / they / go / to the farmers' market / they / buy / organic fruit

   _____

4 if / he / not tilt / the panel / it / generate / less energy

   _____

5 she wishes / she / join / the buyers' cooperative

   _____

6 ? / if / you / visit / the recycling plant / you / seen / the recycling process

   _____

B Complete the sentences with the correct form of these words.

be   have   look after   read   ~~speak~~   take

1 If only we _____ *had spoken* _____ to an expert on renewable sources!

2 I wish everyone _____ the environment like you do!

3 If they _____ a green alternative, they wouldn't have connected to the grid.

4 If only there _____ a farmers' market in our district now.

5 If I _____ the article on global warming, I would have passed the test.

6 I wish she _____ those plastic bottles to the recycling bin yesterday.

C Complete the second sentence so it has the same meaning as the first.

1 We didn't take action quick enough, so the planet is in danger.

   If we _____ *had taken* _____ action quicker, the planet _____ *wouldn't be* _____ in danger.

2 It's a pity we don't have recycling bins.

   If only _____ recycling bins.

3 He didn't realise how effective solar power is, so he didn't turn to it.

   If only he _____ how effective solar power is, he _____ to it.

4 The group wants the government to change its green policies.

   The group wishes the government _____ its green policies.

5 He had been fixing the solar panel when lightening struck.

   If only he _____ the solar panel when lightening struck.

6 He hadn't read the report, so he was embarrassed.

   If he _____ the report, he _____ embarrassed.

Vocabulary

Choose the correct answers.

1 We must put an end to environmental _____ .
   a warming   (b) pollution   c energy

2 Hurricanes, earthquakes and floods are examples of _____ .
   a natural disasters   b high consumption   c nuclear power

3 Drought happens when there is a _____ .
   a dam construction   b water level   c water shortage

4 Wind power is a green _____ to fossil fuels.
   a alternative   b conversion   c grid

5 There has been a population _____ in recent years.
   a construction   b explosion   c management

6 Is photovoltaic energy a(n) _____ source?
   a organic   b global   c renewable

Listening

A 🎧 **Listen to three people talking about issues connected to the environment. Tick (✓) the things they support.**

	cutting down trees	dam construction	complaining	renewable sources	tourism
Speaker 1				✓	
Speaker 2					
Speaker 3					

B 🎧 **Listen and decide whether each statement is right (A) or wrong (B).**

		A	B
1	Daniel Plainview is the actor in *There Will Be Blood*.	☐	☑
2	Erin Brockovich is a real person.	☐	☐
3	A large company caused the pollution in Hinkley.	☐	☐
4	*An Inconvenient Truth* is a cartoon.	☐	☐
5	*An Inconvenient Truth* shows how natural disasters and global warming are connected.	☐	☐
6	In *The Emerald Forest*, Bill Markham is kidnapped.	☐	☐

Speaking

Remember!

When we are predicting we use expressions like these.

If people continue/carry on + -ing ..., there'll ...

Unless people stop + -ing, there'll ...

If we don't take action, it'll ...

Unless we take action, it'll ...

... might/may/will result in + -ing/noun

... might/may/will lead to + bare infinitive/noun

A Look at the pictures in C and the phrases below. Write 1 next to the phrases which we can use to talk about picture 1, 2 next to the phrases we can use to talk about picture 2 and B next to phrases we can use to talk about both pictures.

a doesn't contribute to global warming ☐ 2

b increases environmental pollution ☐

c is bad for people's health ☐

d is expensive ☐

e creates no emissions ☐

f is not efficient enough ☐

g pollutes the environment ☐

h is ugly ☐

i spoils the landscape ☐

B Complete these sentences in your own words.

1 Unless we stop using fossil fuels, there'll _____ .

2 Using renewable sources like wind power might _____ .

3 If we carry on using power stations, there'll _____ .

4 Unless we take action, _____ .

5 Power stations emit _____ .

6 Global warming is caused by _____ .

7 Wind power isn't a good idea because _____ .

C The pictures below show two ways of making energy. Role play an interview about their advantages and disadvantages with your partner. Student A will be the presenter of a radio programme and Student B will be an expert on energy.

1

2

Discussion

What 'small' things can we do every day that will help reduce environmental pollution?

Vocabulary

Circle the correct words.

1 It will highlight / talk existing problems and offer solutions.

2 It will make aims / recommendations about how to get support from local government.

3 Our group has analysed / proven that you can achieve a lot if you try.

4 The 'stay green' project has achieved a great lot / deal.

5 The purpose / suggestion of this report is to suggest new areas of interest for our group.

6 There is no doubt that the campaign has been extremely worthwhile / intended.

Remember!

We use linking words such as these to make our writing flow better.

as, since, because	To show the reason why something happens.
also, as well, and, too, as well as	To join different ideas that are related in some way.
like, such as, for example, for instance	To give examples.

Remember, when we give examples, we can only use **for example** and **for instance** at the start of a sentence. We must use **like** and **such as** in the middle of a sentence.

Model writing task

Read the writing task and the model composition and complete it with these words.

Imagine you want to start up a 'green club' in your school. Write a report for your teachers and fellow students explaining why such a club is necessary and suggesting where and when the club could be held.

also   and   as   For example   like   such

model composition

Report on need for a 'green club'.

Introduction

The aim of this report is to highlight why Chiltern School should set up a 'green club'. It will analyse the reasons why such a club would be beneficial. It will (1) _____also_____ suggest a suitable place and time for the members of the club to meet.

Reasons for establishing the club

There is no doubt that our school, (2) _____ other schools, must have its own club whose members will learn about issues concerning the environment. If students are allowed to take an active part in dealing with problems (3) _____ as pollution, then we could make a difference in our area.

Location and time

• If the school could provide the club with its own room, this would be fantastic. There is an empty room at the moment next to the school library. This room would be ideal for the club (4) _____ it means that we can easily go to the library if we need to use its facilities for the club's activities. (5) _____, we would have access to computers and relevant books.

• Also, I would recommend that the club take place on Tuesdays and Thursdays at 4.30 pm. Since these are days when no other clubs or activities take place, all students will have the chance to become members.

Conclusion

The establishment of green clubs in other schools has proven that when students take responsibility for the environment, they can bring about significant changes. For this reason, I propose that we set up a club like this at our school in the place (6) _____ at the time mentioned above.

Grammar

Match.

1	If they had had a better solution,	a	must we clean it afterwards?
2	Unless more people join the club,	b	if we had asked her?
3	If we want to use this room,	c	they would have mentioned it.
4	Could the mayor have helped	d	please let us know.
5	If you have any recommendations,	e	they may not get it.
6	Should we suggest recycling bins	f	it can't go ahead.
7	If we can do anything to help,	g	if they ask for suggestions?
8	If the groups ask for a lot of money,	h	you can bring them up at the next meeting.

Your writing task

A Read the writing task and number the paragraphs in the correct order.

Imagine a 'green club' has just been started up at your school and a name has been chosen for it. Write a report for your teachers and fellow students. Say what the name is and why it was chosen. Also, suggest the first project that the club could deal with and analyse why the project is important.

Title: Report on 'green club'.

Paragraph [2]   Club's name: discuss the club's name and explain why it was chosen.

Paragraph ☐   Conclusion: make a final statement about the club's name and proposed project.

Paragraph ☐   Introduction: introduce the topic and give the reason for writing.

Paragraph ☐   Proposed project: say which project the club could deal with first and analyse the reasons why.

B Now write your report.

Vocabulary

A Look at the pictures and write the correct phrases.

> Dispose of properly.   Hold someone responsible.   Hold the line.
> Keep a secret.   Keep an account.   Pollute the air.

Dispose of properly.

B Find eight words and use them to complete the sentences.

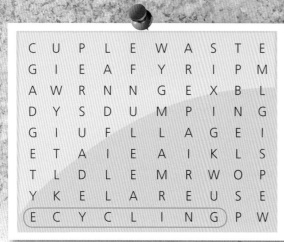

C	U	P	L	E	W	A	S	T	E
G	I	E	A	F	Y	R	I	P	M
A	W	R	N	N	G	E	X	B	L
D	Y	S	D	U	M	P	I	N	G
G	I	U	F	L	L	A	G	E	I
E	T	A	I	E	A	I	K	L	S
T	L	D	L	E	M	R	W	O	P
Y	K	E	L	A	R	E	U	S	E
E	C	Y	C	L	I	N	G	P	W

1   Is there an ____e-cycling____ centre in your district?
2   Throwing away electronic goods creates _____ .
3   Sam plays with this _____ all the time.
4   I can't _____ the headmaster to recycle paper.
5   This _____ full of rubbish smells terrible.
6   The TV is broken and I can't _____ it.
7   _____ rubbish is not allowed here.
8   We should always try to _____ things instead of throwing them away.

C Match.

1   Don't hold your
2   The problem with waste can be relieved
3   Dangerous substances have leaked
4   The council have kept their
5   It's not expensive to process
6   I disagree with the opinion

a   by e-cycling.
b   word by dealing with air pollution.
c   breath for big changes.
d   electronic waste.
e   he holds on landfills.
f   into the river.

Grammar

A Complete the paragraph with the gerund or full infinitive formed from the verbs in brackets.

In recent years, most electronics manufacturers have made an effort (1) _____ to adopt _____ (adopt) a take-back policy for their goods. However, the problem of e-waste continues (2) _____ (grow) daily. The question is, should these companies be forced (3) _____ (accept) all the responsibility for this waste? Another idea worth (4) _____ (consider) is fining consumers. Local governments could fine people for (5) _____ (throw away) electronic goods that are in working condition. This is a solution which may be difficult (6) _____ (enforce), but may give people the incentive (7) _____ (dispose) of waste more carefully. If we don't stop (8) _____ (pollute) our environment, we will all pay sooner or later.

B Complete the sentences using a gerund or full infinitive and any other words necessary.

1   Electronics companies shouldn't be allowed _____ .
2   We should begin _____ .
3   It's no use _____ .
4   Not everyone can resist the temptation _____ .
5   I have a laptop that's too old _____ .
6   I don't feel like _____ .

C Circle the sentence, a or b, that means the same as the first sentence.

1   Shipping waste abroad isn't effective.
   (a) It's no use sending waste abroad.
   b   Waste from foreign ships isn't effective.
2   He didn't remember to dispose of the mobile properly.
   a   He disposed of the mobile properly but forgets doing it.
   b   He forgot to dispose of the mobile properly.
3   She went on to tell us about the e-cycling plant.
   a   She talked about nothing else but the e-cycling plant.
   b   She changed her topic of conversation to the e-cycling plant.
4   They have stopped dumping in this landfill.
   a   They don't dump in this landfill any more.
   b   They got out of the car to dump rubbish in this landfill.
5   Have you been meaning to swap this TV?
   a   Do you have the intention of swapping this TV?
   b   Can you explain swapping this TV to me?
6   They forgot to advertise the take-back policy.
   a   They didn't advertise the take-back policy because they didn't remember to.
   b   They advertised the take-back policy, but don't remember doing it.

Lesson 2

Vocabulary

A Circle the odd one out.

1 cash card	(Velcro)	PIN
2 draw	imitate	mimic
3 prickly	inspired	motivated
4 cable	theory	principle
5 boxfish	komodo dragon	memory stick
6 firmly	extremely	securely

B Circle the correct words.

1 This fabric was based on a cat's (coat) / fastener.

2 The new submarine is shaped as / like a ball.

3 I pay my bills at the cash point / money box.

4 We really respect her like / as an engineer.

5 The fish got caught on the hook / loop.

6 Does this fish cut across / through water efficiently?

C Complete the paragraph with these words.

acted   available   dressed   hi-tech   looked   make   wacky   worked

Modern technology has always fascinated me. When I was young, I used to take my toy cars to pieces because I wanted to see what all the parts (1) _____looked_____ like. I used to tell people that I (2) _____ as a mechanic and I even (3) _____ up as one sometimes in my uncle's overalls! My brothers used to tease me, however, and say that I was (4) _____ . They would tell me it'd be better if I (5) _____ like the other girls more. But I knew that it was OK for girls to want to be mechanics too. I still believe it's important for everyone to make use of the opportunities (6) _____ to them. My childhood dream has come true and today it's my job to study nature and use this knowledge to design (7) _____ gadgets that (8) _____ a profit for the company I work for.

Grammar

A Complete the sentences with these words.

> as to   for   in case   ~~in order to~~   so that   to

1 Let's go into the bank _____ *in order to* _____ ask for a new PIN.
2 Take your cash card _____ they ask you for it.
3 They studied flies _____ they could learn from their wings.
4 They stopped his credit card _____ no good reason.
5 He spoke to the researcher _____ ask for his advice.
6 They imitated a leaf so _____ make waterproof paint.

B Join the sentences using the words in brackets.

1 He bought a memory stick. He wanted to transfer data to his home computer. (so as to)
   He bought a memory stick so as to transfer data to his home computer.

2 They used Velcro. They wanted to hold the cables together. (to)
   _____

3 She went to the cash point. She wanted to take out some money. (so that)
   _____

4 We designed the car to mimic a fish. We wanted to make it go faster. (in order to)
   _____

5 They did the research again. They didn't want to have been wrong the first time. (in case)
   _____

6 I looked online. I wanted to buy a DVD player. (for)
   _____

C Look at the pictures and write T (true) or F (false).

1 He put on glasses in order to protect his eyes. ☐ T
2 She didn't answer the phone in case she had an accident. ☐
3 They used trucks so as to clear the snow. ☐
4 She went to the office to work. ☐
5 She touched the screen so that she would be recognised. ☐
6 She only uses her mobile phone for text messages. ☐

Vocabulary

Circle the correct words.

1 Here, put my (earphones) / binoculars on to listen to this!
2 Dad really wants a DVD / GPS unit for his birthday.
3 The games console / printer has run out of paper.
4 Hassan bought a new home cinema / music centre so he can watch all his favourite films.
5 This camcorder / digital camera doesn't take photos, only videos.
6 I didn't realise you had a microwave oven / an electric piano. Can I play it, please?

Listening

A 🎧 **Listen and number the favourite things in the correct order.**

a games console ☐
b microwave oven ☐
c MP3 player ☐
d electric piano ☐
e GPS unit ☐ 1
f digital camera ☐

B 🎧 **Listen and tick (✓) the correct pictures.**

1 What is the man looking for?

a  b  c  ✓

2 How much do the binoculars cost?

a 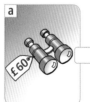 £60 b  £35.60 c  £89

3 What did the woman receive for her birthday?

a  b  c

4 What time is the film showing?

a  b  c

5 Who will give the talk?

a  b  c

6 What has the engineer already invented?

a 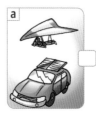 b 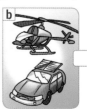 c

Speaking

A Write MP (mobile phone), D (DVD player), B (binoculars), G (games console) and MC (music centre) in the boxes to show how often you use each piece of equipment from task C.

every day	
a few times a week	
once a week	
a few times a month	
a few times a year	
never	

Remember!

When we're giving advice, we use expressions like these.
If it was me, I'd + bare infinitive ...
If I was in his/her shoes, I'd + bare infinitive ...
He/She ought to/should + bare infinitive ...
He/She would be better + ing
Why don't we suggest he/she ...?
My advice would be + full infinitive ...
I think you should warn/point out/ talk about/discuss ...

B Read the task in C and then read part of a dialogue between two students who are doing the task. Complete the dialogue with phrases from the *Remember!* box.

Katie: (1) _____ If it was me/If I was in his shoes _____, I'd choose the binoculars because I love them.

Lee: But not all young people would agree. (2) _____ to choose objects that are used by most or all students.

Katie: Yes, OK. (3) _____ putting in the mobile phone?

Lee: I agree and I think we (4) _____ that we use them to communicate with others and to listen to music.

Katie: That's a good idea. (5) _____ that he chooses a games console too?

Lee: I'm not sure about that. (6) _____ pick a DVD player, I think.

C The headmaster at your school has been asked to fill a box with objects that will show people in the future how young people today use technology. Work with a partner to discuss how suitable the objects below are and recommend two you think should definitely be included.

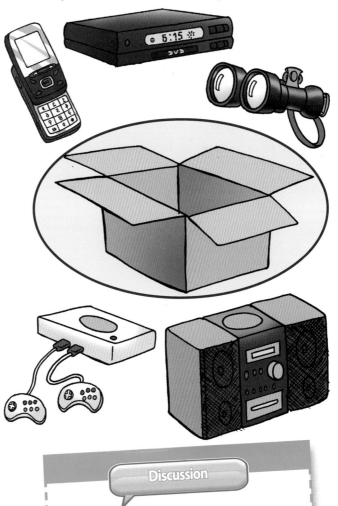

Discussion

How strict must parents be with:
a their children using the internet?
b their children playing games on consoles?

Vocabulary

Put the words in the correct order to make sentences.

1   am / an / owed / I / feel / explanation / I
    I feel I am owed an explanation.

2   your / I / complain / to / writing / am / about / product
    _____
    _____

3   is / utterly / this / I / unacceptable / believe
    _____
    _____

4   this / deal / I / immediately / you / with / expect / to / matter
    _____
    _____

5   service / am / your / extremely / I / with / disappointed
    _____
    _____

6   insist / a / I / refund / on / complete / money / my / of
    _____
    _____

Remember!

Linking words or phrases show how a sentence or paragraph relates to the previous one. We use words and phrases like:

in addition, moreover	to add information
as a result, consequently, therefore, this means that	to show result
first of all, secondly, finally	to order information
despite, however, on the other hand	to show contrast

Model writing task

Read the writing task and the model composition and circle the correct words.

You recently bought a DVD player after seeing the advert below. However, there are several problems with it and you want a refund. Use your notes on the advert to write an email complaining about it.

DVD player is 7 inches, screen's only 5

I didn't get this.

It's too small for the DVD player.

Now you can watch your favourite films on the move with the Pirrips portable DVD player!

DVD features:
- 7 inch screen
- battery lasts for up to 5 hours
- 2 headphone inputs so 2 people can watch at the same time
- remote control included
- weighs only 850 grams

Order now while stocks last!

Free case with every order placed by 28th February

I was charged £15 extra!

Was £95
Now £70!
Save £15!

model composition

Dear Sir/Madam,

I am writing to complain about the Pirrips DVD player I bought from your company last week. I am extremely disappointed with the product and your company and I would like you to refund my money.

(1) First of all / Secondly, in your advert you say that the DVD player has got a 7 inch screen.

(2) Therefore / However, I found that although the DVD player is 7 inches across the actual screen is only 5 inches.

(3) On the other hand / This means that it is very difficult to see what is happening on the screen. I believe this is utterly unacceptable as I chose this DVD player specifically due to the size of the screen. Furthermore,

(4) consequently / despite the fact the advert promises a remote control with each player, I did not receive one.

(5) Moreover / Firstly, I feel that your company is unreliable. The price quoted in your advert was fifteen pounds cheaper than the original price, however, I was charged fifteen pounds extra online. I would also like to point out that the DVD case that you advertise as a free gift is far too small for the DVD player.

(6) To conclude / In addition, I insist on a full refund of the money I paid for this product. I also expect your company to have its advert changed, or else I will take the matter further.

Yours faithfully,
Ina Huph

Grammar

A Complete the sentences with the causative form using the words given and the tense in brackets.

1 They ___are having/getting the recycling plant painted___ next week. (the recycling plant / paint)
  (Present Continuous)

2 She _____ her car when I spoke to her. (a new CD player /
  not put in) (Past Perfect Simple)

3 The inventor _____ tomorrow. (his tooth / remove)
  (Future Simple)

4 He _____ every year. (the solar panel / check) (Present Simple)

5 Anne _____ by the author. (the book / sign) (Past Simple)

B Complete the sentences with the correct form of **have** or **get**. Sometimes both verbs can be used.

1 Charles _____had/got_____ his new electric piano delivered last Thursday.

2 We _____ our microwave oven stolen when we moved house.

3 They _____ a planetarium built in their garden at the moment.

4 She _____ her GPS unit repaired twice this month.

5 Gran _____ photovoltaic panels installed on her roof since 9 am.

Your writing task

A Read the writing task and correct the words in bold in the model plan.

You recently bought a games console after seeing the advert below for it. However, there are several problems with the games console and you want a replacement. Use your notes on the advert to write an email complaining about it.

Mine only has 20 games

no batteries were included

mine was broken

They wouldn't take mine because it wasn't a Mexall.

Play all your favourite interactive games with the Mexall Games Console!

Console features:
- programmed with 40 interactive games
- batteries included
- 1 controller included
- weighs only 5 kgs

Was £150
Now £120!
Save £30!

Take-back policy on all old consoles – no matter what make!

Greeting: ~~Hi~~ Dear Sir/Madam,
Paragraph 1:   State your reason for **calling**.
Paragraph 2:   Discuss why you **liked** the product.
Paragraph 3:   Discuss another problem with the product.
Paragraph 4:   Discuss a problem with the service you **gave**.
Paragraph 5:   Ask for a **refund**.

B Now write your email.

Review 4

Reading

A Read the article about an Alternative Energy Fair.

Green power

It started off as an electric car race in the late 1990s. Today it has developed into one of the US's most important exhibitions of green energy alternatives and how they can be used. The Alternative Energy Fair, which is held in Washington's Huntamer Park, has even been given an award for excellence.

In 2008, the fair became one of Washington's biggest events dealing with renewable energy. Visitors to the fair include people who want to check out green alternatives for their home energy supply, for their cars or even for their place of work. They can find information on how to save energy by replacing light bulbs right down to which materials they should use to build their houses in order to make them use and lose less energy.

On display at the fair for visitors to admire are all sorts of green innovations. Driving a car which runs on electricity converted by a photovoltaic panel on the roof may seem like science fiction, but the fair shows that it is possible. We might not be able to take these cars for a test drive at the moment, however it may be only a matter of time before we can.

The residents of Washington will no doubt be among the first to do so. Electric cars which use energy from renewable sources can already be seen on the city's roads. There are even electric vehicle charging stations in the city so that drivers who've gone green can recharge their batteries.

It's easy to see why the US Environmental Protection Agency has officially called Lacey, the area where Huntamer Park is found, a Green Power Community. The lights in public parks and public buildings, the street lamps and traffic lights all work using 100% green energy.

Green power is without a doubt the way forward. With fossil fuels running out rapidly and global warming becoming one of the world's most serious problems, other towns and cities ought to follow this example. Turning to renewable sources for our energy needs is the only sensible choice we have to help our environment.

B Write A if the sentence is correct and B if it is not correct.

1. In the late 1990s Huntamer Park received an award. `B`
2. The fair informs people about saving energy.
3. Cars with a photovoltaic panel are one of the objects that have appeared in the fair.
4. It is possible to take a photovoltaic car for a test drive at the fair.
5. Some people in Washington already drive electric cars.
6. All the public buildings in Lacey have lights using 100% green energy.

Vocabulary

Choose the correct answers.

1 We always knew Albert would be a high _____ .
   a flyer
   b fastener
   c researcher

2 We're all holding our _____ for their latest invention.
   a principle
   b vision
   c breath

3 Toxic waste is _____ into our drinking water!
   a releasing
   b emitting
   c leaking

4 I was able to transfer all the files to my _____ .
   a sensor
   b memory stick
   c cable

5 Please _____ and I'll put you through to Steve.
   a keep an account
   b refresh your memory
   c hold the line

6 These researchers are famous for their _____ .
   a shortage
   b excellence
   c extinction

7 Gamal is well _____ as a biologist.
   a respected
   b acted
   c imitated

8 You must remember your _____ and never tell it to anyone.
   a PIN
   b USB
   c GPS

9 Engineering isn't my strong _____ .
   a scratch
   b device
   c point

10 What _____ global warming?
   a ran out
   b brought about
   c drew out

11 The company have won three awards for design and _____ .
   a innovation
   b prediction
   c conversion

12 High _____ of energy is a big problem.
   a grid
   b consumption
   c explosion

Grammar

Choose the correct answers.

1 The researcher stopped _____ have a break.
   a so as
   b for
   c to

2 _____ a photovoltaic car helps the environment.
   a Driving
   b To drive
   c Drive

3 _____ I had a printer!
   a When
   b If only
   c Wish

4 When the temperature _____ , snow melts.
   a will rise
   b rises
   c would rise

5 If I _____ an inventor, I'd look to nature for inspiration.
   a am
   b would be
   c were

6 She would convert to a renewable source if she _____ .
   a might
   b could
   c must

7 They _____ their laptop stolen last month.
   a had
   b got
   c were

8 _____ we learn much if we study the snow leopard?
   a Will
   b Would
   c Should

9 Bring your cash card _____ need more money.
   a so that we
   b to
   c in case we

10 We _____ to the laboratory because we were hungry.
   a got delivered a pizza
   b got a pizza delivered
   c delivered a pizza

11 Our planet will be in greater danger _____ we consume less energy.
   a unless
   b if
   c if only

12 _____ waste into rivers shouldn't be allowed.
   a To dump
   b Dumping
   c Dump

Vocabulary

A Complete the sentences with these words.

> graduation   grant   income   ~~overtime~~   recession

1 I can't come out tonight because I have to work _____ *overtime* _____ .
2 You should apply for a(n) _____ if you want to study at university.
3 The _____ has meant that many families can't afford holidays anymore.
4 You can increase your _____ by doing a second job.
5 What do you plan to do after _____?

B Complete the crossword puzzle.

Across

3 You make somebody this when you tell them they must leave their job.

4 You do this when you learn to do something new and different.

6 You do this when you cut down on spending.

Down

1 People feel awkward when you do this to them.

2 You do this when you receive a degree from college or university.

5 You do this when you try to get a job.

Crossword letters:
1 (down) E M B A R R A S S
2 (down) G
3 (across) R
4 (across) R
5 (across) A
6 (across) E

C Choose the correct words.

1 Ryan is studying for his _____ exam.
   a economist
   b accountant
   c economics ←(circled)

2 The _____ sent a small van for our furniture.
   a estate agent
   b removals company
   c applicant

3 It's important to be _____ of relatives who're unemployed.
   a worried
   b supportive
   c concerned

4 We're managing to _____ up with our payments.
   a keep
   b take
   c put

5 Please submit a recent photo with your _____ .
   a job-hunting
   b application
   c embarrassment

6 Their lack of free time is putting a huge _____ on their friendship.
   a strain
   b mortgage
   c treat

Grammar

A Circle the correct words.

1 She (told)/ said / told to her parents her graduation was in July.

2 Ray said he had felt / feels / felt embarrassed when the estate agent arrived unexpectedly.

3 Martha told me she had already applied / already applies / applied already for the position.

4 The bank has said they must / had to / should have pay their mortgage tomorrow.

5 The student said he looked / looks / was looking for a part-time job.

B Complete the second sentences using reported speech.

1 'Ricky didn't get the job.'
The manager said _____ (that) Ricky didn't get/hadn't got the job _____ .

2 'We're not hiring new people this year.'
The company owner said _____ .

3 'You ought to go on a training programme.'
The careers advisor told _____ .

4 'The successful applicant will be informed by email.'
Last month she said _____ .

5 'You can speak to my accountant tomorrow.'
Saleh told _____ .

C Complete the paragraph to report the dialogue.

Careers advisor:	Hi Pete. I hear you want some information about becoming an estate agent.
Pete:	That's right. I have a friend who's an estate agent and he'll give me a job if I have the appropriate qualifications.
Careers advisor:	Well, I did some research and it looks like successful estate agents need a good knowledge of numbers. So you might want to think about studying accounts or economics.
Pete:	That's what my friend says. I was planning to apply to college to do accounts.
Careers advisor:	That's a good idea. You could also ask your friend to give you a Saturday job so that you can see what the job involves.
Pete:	I hadn't thought of that. I'll give him a call tonight.

Pete went to see the careers advisor yesterday. She said that she (1) _____ had heard he wanted _____ some information on becoming an estate agent. Pete told her that (2) _____ an estate agent and that (3) _____ give him a job if he had the appropriate qualifications. The careers advisor said that she (4) _____ some research. She (5) _____ that successful estate agents need a good knowledge of numbers. She then told Pete that he (6) _____ studying accounts or economics. Pete told her he (7) _____ to go to college to do accounts. The careers advisor approved of his decision and also said he (8) _____ for a Saturday job so he could see what the job involves. Pete said that he (9) _____ and that he (10) _____ .

79

Vocabulary

A **Circle the correct words.**

1 Brian, Claire and John went on the all-female / underwater mission.

2 His research on marine life was absolutely solo / outstanding.

3 We've put upon / together a list of all accountants in the area.

4 I've just got into / enrolled the best college in Paris!

5 There are no current vocations / vacancies for cleaners.

6 Our teacher hates it when we call him by his nickname / scholarship.

B **Complete the dialogue with these words.**

conditions	expertise	mind	mission	researcher	ropes

Dad: Hi, Mo. How was your first day at work?

Mo: Alright, I suppose, Dad. I didn't really do much to be honest. Ms Tatler showed me the (1) _____ropes_____ and I mostly watched the others working. Pretty dull really.

Dad: Well, when you're working in dangerous (2) _____ like you will be, it's important to take time to see how to do things properly.

Mo: I know, but I'm not sure there'll be any danger. I mean, when I applied for the job, I thought that as an assistant to an underwater (3) _____ I'd at least get to go out in a boat or even do some diving.

Dad: They wouldn't have you going on a(n) (4) _____ on your first day, Mo!

Mo: I don't think I'll ever be going on one. It looks like I'll be stuck in the laboratory helping Ms Tatler with her research.

Dad: You know, it brings to (5) _____ my first day at work. I remember feeling disappointed too that I wasn't given enough to do and it wasn't exciting enough. But you must remember that you've got years ahead of you. This was only one day and each day you'll do more and learn more. Slowly you'll acquire more and more knowledge until your (6) _____ on underwater research becomes well known.

Mo: I guess you're telling me to take it a day at a time.

Dad: Exactly!

C **Match.**

1 All employees should feel   a out to be a diver.

2 Are you coming   b the world record for running 100 m?

3 He's afraid of deep water so he's not cut   c data the best part of the job.

4 Do you know who holds   d along on the field trip?

5 I find gathering   e upon all employees with respect.

6 The boss looks   f free to take regular breaks.

Grammar

A **Write the sentences in reported speech.**

1 'Ask them for funding for the project,' Mr Watt told us.
   Mr Watt told us to ask them for funding for the project.

2 'Have they finished the basic training?' Nancy asked.

3 'What time do you start in the morning?' Mum asked me.

4 'Can we come along on the tour of the factory?' the employees asked.

5 'Take the rest of the day off,' the boss told us.

6 'Please may I enrol on this course?' Suzie asked.

B **Write what the people said.**

1 The secretary told Mr Mathews to take a seat.
   (Please) take a seat, Mr Mathews.

2 Pam asked if they should check to see if there were any current vacancies.

3 We asked who was in charge of the mission.

4 The employee told me to hold the line.

5 The doctor asked where the problem was.

6 I asked my boss what I should do next.

C **Find and correct six errors.**

Last week I went for a job interview for a position as a truck driver. When I arrived I was shown into a small room and asked ~~if~~ do a quick test. Most of the questions were very difficult and weren't related to the job I had applied for, but I tried my best. After half an hour a man called Mr Jenkins came into the room and asked me who I had finished the test. He told me to wait outside in the hall and to not talk to any of the other people who had come for an interview. I had been waiting for about five minutes when one of the others approached me. He asked me to tell him whether the test was about. I told him I couldn't say anything and I asked him not to insist. Just then Mr Jenkins came out of the room and asked what everything was OK and told me go to his office. I tried to explain what had happened, but he said that it was alright as it had been part of the test. He offered me the job, but I wasn't sure if I wanted it any more!

Vocabulary

Circle the odd one out.

1 supervisor	manager	~~bricklayer~~
2 overalls	hard hat	blueprints
3 goggles	electrician	protective gloves
4 steel-toe capped boots	drill	manual worker
5 carpenter	vocation	civil engineer

Listening

A 🎧 **Listen to the three people talking about their jobs and complete the table.**

	Current job	Number of years	Future plans
Speaker 1	(1) _____carpenter_____	(2) _____	part-time (3) _____
Speaker 2	(4) _____	(5) _____	her own (6) _____
Speaker 3	(7) _____	(8) _____	create a (9) _____

B 🎧 **You will hear two people talking about equipment employees require. Which object does each person need? For questions 1-5, write a letter (A-H) next to each person. There are three letters which you do not need to use.**

1 Kim   [H]
2 Marion   ☐
3 Stavros   ☐
4 Pierre   ☐
5 Ron   ☐

A   drill
B   goggles
C   protective gloves
D   overalls
E   tool belt
F   hard hat
G   blueprints
H   steel-toe capped boots

Speaking

A Choose one picture of a man and one picture of a woman from C. Write as many words as you can think of related to each picture you have chosen.

Picture 1	Picture 2
_____	_____
_____	_____
_____	_____
_____	_____
_____	_____

Remember!

When we are talking about work, we use expressions like these.

They're on a construction site/in an office/ a classroom/a warehouse/a factory.

The working conditions are dangerous/ extremely difficult/excellent/fairly good.

He/She's wearing protective clothing/ a uniform/casual clothes/a suit.

He/She's in charge of ...

He/She works with his/her hands.

It's a highly skilled/low-skilled job.

Job titles include:

apprentice	supervisor
manager	trainee
manual worker	trainer

B Write short descriptions of the people you chose in A. Use sentences from the *Remember!* box to help you.

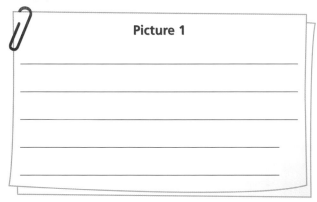

Picture 1

_____
_____
_____
_____
_____

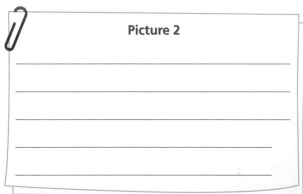

Picture 2

_____
_____
_____
_____
_____

C Work with a partner. Spend one minute describing one of the people in the pictures and then ask your partner who you are describing. Student A will describe a man and student B will describe a woman.

Discussion

'Parents shouldn't interfere in their children's choice of career.' Discuss.

Vocabulary

Circle the correct words.

1   At beginning /(first) it was the perfect job.
2   At the end of the while / day, she realised she had been foolish.
3   Ken has just got his big lifetime / break.
4   Just then / Looking back, a student rushed in.
5   The manager screamed at him politely / nastily.

Remember!

A successful short story must not have more than 2-3 characters. It should have an interesting plot, and a clear beginning, middle and end. Good short-story writers use several means to capture readers' interest and make them continue reading. These include using dramatic opening sentences, descriptive adjectives and adverbs, direct speech, short dramatic sentences and sometimes an unexpected twist in the plot.

Model writing task

Read the writing task and the model composition and say how the writer has captured the readers' interest or ordered events in the highlighted parts.

Write a story with the title The dishonest employee.

model composition

The dishonest employee

dramatic opening sentence
It was late on a cold, rainy Friday evening and everyone just wanted to go home. The manager, Mr Smith, had gathered everyone together beside the checkouts. He had an important announcement to make and he didn't look at all happy.

At first, Sasha feared that they were about to be told the company was closing. The recession had hit a lot of companies in the area, so she was prepared to hear the worst. Just then, Mr Smith spoke in an angry voice.

'I'll get straight to the point. One of you is stealing!' he exclaimed pointing his finger accusingly at all the employees. 'Money has been going missing for a month now.' He warned everyone that they were suspects. He then promised it wouldn't be long before he found the guilty person.

After that, nothing was the same again for Sasha and her colleagues at the supermarket. There was a horrible atmosphere as nobody knew who they could trust anymore. Employees even started spying on each other.

A few weeks later, the owner of the supermarket turned up unexpectedly. The employees were sure the thief had been found. Surprisingly, Mr Smith was absent. The owner explained that Mr Smith had been sacked for mismanagement.

Looking back, it was obvious Mr Smith was too blame all along. He was the only one who controlled the money. He had made some bad decisions and blamed the staff for the company's losses. Sasha was relieved that it was over. She was even more relieved that Mr Smith hadn't managed to get someone else fired for his dishonesty.

Grammar

A The words in bold are wrong. Write the correct words.

1 'I won't steal again.'

He **threatened** that he wouldn't steal again.   _____promised_____

2 'I won't work without being paid!'

She **denied** to work without being paid.   _____

3 'We're sorry for the mistake with your order.'

They **boasted about** the mistake with my order.   _____

4 'Please, please, please give us a pay rise.'

They **admitted to** a pay rise.   _____

5 'Would you like this desk by the window?'

He **refused** her the desk by the window.   _____

6 'It was you who broke the drill.'

He **reminded** me of breaking the drill.   _____

B Complete the second sentence so that it reports the first. Use the words in bold.

1 'Be here on time or I won't pay you.'   **threatened**

The boss _____threatened not to pay me_____ if I wasn't there on time.

2 'Take this package to the warehouse before you go home.'   **ordered**

The manager _____ package to the warehouse before I went home.

3 'Yes, I'll do overtime if necessary.'   **agreed**

I _____ if necessary.

4 'Don't forget the office party is next Thursday.'   **reminded**

She _____ office party was the following Thursday.

5 'You switch off the electricity by pressing this button.'   **explained**

She _____ the electricity.

6 'Why don't you all come to the staff canteen for lunch?'   **invited**

The boss _____ to the staff canteen for lunch.

Your writing task

A Read the writing task and complete the story plan with the words in the box.

Write a story with the title An unusual boss.

| comment | details | events | scene | twist |

Title: An unusual boss

Paragraph 1:   Set the _____scene_____ and introduce the main characters.

Paragraph 2:   Give background _____ to an important event in the story.

Paragraph 3:   Describe the main _____ in detail.

Paragraph 4:   Introduce a(n) _____ in the story.

Paragraph 5:   Bring the story to an end and make a final _____ about the boss.

B Now write your story.

Vocabulary

A Complete the sentences with these words.

| caught | collided | put | tackled | taken |

1 George is being _____ taken _____ to court for careless driving.
2 Firefighters _____ the fire for over two hours.
3 The whole station has been _____ on stand-by.
4 Two trains _____ with each other in Darlington this morning.
5 The robber was _____ red-handed leaving the bank.

B Circle the correct words.

1 He almost died when his breathing / cutting apparatus didn't work.
2 We've been ordered to put all paramedics / casualties on stand-by.
3 Who's conducting the task / investigation into the accident?
4 Don't set blaze / fire to those papers!
5 Luckily the fire was answered / put out in half an hour.
6 Two people were pulled from the wreck / false alarm.

C Find eight emergency-related words and complete the sentences.

S	T	O	H	M	T	R	I	C	K	Q
F	B	L	A	R	S	O	A	Q	P	C
S	E	D	Z	T	B	J	S	N	S	O
F	B	T	A	S	L	E	A	L	A	M
O	K	A	R	S	O	N	I	S	T	M
D	I	I	D	A	N	O	R	T	E	A
E	X	T	I	N	G	U	I	S	H	N
X	P	I	U	Q	S	N	N	U	P	D
C	O	M	M	J	I	S	G	I	O	E
V	R	A	R	E	T	P	R	B	M	R
I	G	S	C	T	N	H	O	A	X	L
O	A	D	V	N	X	R	A	E	Y	P
G	E	P	W	Q	V	B	D	R	A	C

1 Leaving towels on the cooker is a fire _____ hazard _____ .
2 The _____ called all the firefighters into her office.
3 Let's take the _____ because there's an accident in the town centre.
4 We caught the _____ red-handed.
5 Those kids are playing a _____ on the emergency services.
6 We put out the blaze using a _____ .
7 We rushed to the scene but it was a _____ as there was no fire.
8 They're hoping to _____ the fire soon.

Grammar

A Complete the sentences with the passive voice. Use the verbs given and the tense in brackets.

1 The police officer _____*was given*_____ the day off. (give) (Past Simple)

2 Six fires _____ by midday. (report) (Past Perfect Simple)

3 The pumps _____ every week. (check) (Present Simple)

4 The casualty _____ from the car when we arrived. (lift) (Past Continuous)

5 Protective gloves _____ by the firefighters. (wear) (Present Simple)

6 Three calls _____ about an accident in Islington. (make) (Present Perfect Simple)

7 How many emergencies _____ we _____ by three o'clock?
(deal with) (Future Perfect Simple)

8 The thief _____ yet. (not catch) (Present Perfect Simple)

B Change these sentences from passive to active voice.

1 The emergency services will be contacted by the mayor.

   The mayor will contact the emergency services.

2 How to avoid domestic fires is being explained by the commander.

   _____

3 Investigations are conducted by the police into all crimes.

   _____

4 The trick was played by local children.

   _____

5 Four casualties have been treated by paramedics.

   _____

6 The cutting equipment had been damaged in a storm.

   _____

C Choose the correct answers.

1 The curator _____ outside the museum.
   a was photographed
   b photographed
   c been photographed

2 The stolen jewellery was _____ in a bin.
   a finding
   b to find
   c found

3 The blaze was _____ by experienced firefighters.
   a tackle
   b tackled
   c tackling

4 Who _____ the task of informing the relatives?
   a has been given
   b has given
   c gives

5 The ring road _____ cleared as soon as possible.
   a to be
   b will
   c will be

6 _____ criminals punished severely in his court?
   a Do
   b Have
   c Are

87

Vocabulary

A **Write the missing letters.**

1 This is the number of people who have died in an emergency.   d e a t h t o l l

2 This is when people are told to leave an area because of an emergency.   e _ _ _ _ _ _ _ _ _

3 Something you must do is this.   c _ _ _ _ _ _ _ _ _

4 These are people who help in an emergency.   r _ _ _ _ _ w _ _ _ _ _ _

5 This is the feeling of happiness you have when something bad has not happened.   r _ _ _ _ _

6 This is an area destroyed in an emergency.   d _ _ _ _ _ _ _ z _ _ _

B **Choose the correct answers.**

1 The emergency services couldn't do their job due to ineffective _____ .
   a essentials
   b co-ordination
   c agencies

2 Let's get the survivors to _____ as quickly as possible.
   a shock
   b position
   c safety

3 _____ the patient's condition for another 48 hours.
   a Battle
   b Monitor
   c Flock

4 They must _____ the rescue plan into action immediately.
   a put
   b pump
   c get

5 Never put your head _____ if you have a nosebleed.
   a still
   b back
   c out

6 The storm _____ overnight and helicopters moved people to high ground.
   a intensified
   b declared
   c evacuated

C **Circle the correct words.**

1 We put / got a shock when we saw the town after the flood.

2 There are still thousands of people missing / managing after the disaster.

3 If you are ever on / in doubt, ask the commander.

4 Should we get / put him in a different position?

5 The residents live in / for fear of another storm.

6 We've never been involved in such a large-scale / tropical rescue mission.

Grammar

A Change the sentences from active to passive voice.

1 They always make casualties stay in hospital overnight.
   Casualties are always made to stay in hospital overnight.

2 We couldn't pump out all the water.
   _____

3 The authorities should have monitored the area.
   _____

4 Someone saw him standing on a roof.
   _____

5 They wanted to evacuate Jane, but she refused.
   _____

6 They were supposed to declare a state of emergency yesterday.
   _____

B Write questions in the passive and short answers.

1 he / complain about / not inform / of the situation / yesterday ✓
   Did he complain about not being informed of the situation yesterday?   _Yes, he did._

2 she / always hate / take / to hospital ✓
   _____   _____

3 they / should / warned / about the accident ✗
   _____   _____

4 the casualty / see / take / medicines / this morning ✗
   _____   _____

5 the essentials / should / deliver / at 10 am ✓
   _____   _____

6 the wound / can / treat / now ✓
   _____   _____

C Complete the second sentences using the words in bold. Use between two and five words.

1 The police are chasing the escaped prisoner and he doesn't like it. **by**
   The escaped prisoner doesn't like _____ _being chased by_ _____ the police.

2 They will need to use cutting equipment to free the injured man. **must**
   Cutting equipment _____ to free the injured man.

3 They should make an effort to rescue the dogs. **be**
   An effort _____ to rescue the dogs.

4 The authorities made the residents abandon their homes. **to**
   The residents _____ their homes by the authorities.

5 The doctor asked me to put my head back. **was**
   I _____ my head back by the doctor.

6 She was surprised at receiving an award for bravery. **given**
   She was surprised at _____ for bravery.

Vocabulary

Circle the correct words.

1 (Joyriding) / Joyfulness is a crime against property.

2 Dangerous criminals should receive a warning / prison sentence.

3 A young offenders' institution / Community service is like a prison for people under 18.

4 After the earthquake the town was a disaster zone / death toll.

5 Traffic / Nuclear accidents are common near our local supermarket.

6 People who dump rubbish illegally should be made to pay a fine / an evacuation.

Listening

A 🎧 **Listen and number the pictures in the correct order.**

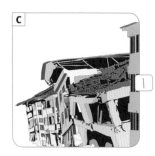

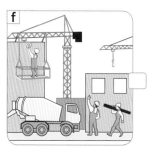

B 🎧 **Listen and choose the correct answers.**

1 How many pets have gone missing?
   a two
   b three
   (c) ten

2 People can call *Crime Busters* from
   a 7.15.
   b 10.30.
   c 12.00.

3 Humphry John
   a has been a firefighter for a year.
   b has researched incidents of arson.
   c has been responsible for over 6,000 fires.

4 Which punishment did the joyriders not receive today?
   a community service
   b driving license removed
   c prison sentence

5 Police Chief Alison Saunders
   a is in a local police station.
   b appears on *Crime Busters*.
   c always solves crimes on the programme.

6 The presenter encourages viewers to call
   a with any information they may have.
   b only when they're positive they can help.
   c and leave their name and address.

Speaking

A Look at the pictures in C and complete the table. Rank the crimes from 1 (least serious) to 5 (most serious) and suggest a suitable punishment.

	Crime	Rank	Punishment
1	arson/lighting forest fire	☐	_____
2	_____	☐	_____
3	_____	☐	_____
4	_____	☐	_____
5	_____	☐	_____
6	_____	☐	_____

Remember!

When we are giving our opinion we use expressions like these.
I believe/think …
In my opinion, …
The way I see it, …
To my mind, …
I'd suggest they receive …
My advice is for them to …

When we are presenting arguments we use expressions like these.
… is/isn't a crime young people commit often.
… is a much more serious crime/ issue than …
… isn't as serious as …, but it's common among …
… is a crime against property/ a person, so …

B Complete these sentences in your own words.

1 In my opinion, armed robbery _____ .
2 _____ is a much more serious crime than shoplifting.
3 Vandalism is a crime against property, so _____ .
4 The way I see it, people who light forest fires _____ .
5 I'd suggest burglars receive _____ .
6 To my mind, a fine is the most appropriate punishment for _____ .

C Look at the pictures below and discuss with a partner how serious these crimes and issues are and what punishments are appropriate for the people who commit them.

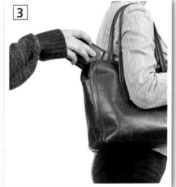

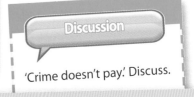

Discussion

'Crime doesn't pay.' Discuss.

Vocabulary

Complete the sentences with these words.

| commented | conducted | eyewitness | regulations | rushed | scene |

1 In spite of safety _____ regulations _____, the building caught fire.
2 A(n) _____ provided a detailed description of the burglar.
3 Authorities have _____ a full investigation of the incident.
4 Six casualties were _____ to the local hospital.
5 Police arrived on the _____ just as the fight started.
6 A hospital spokesperson later _____ that the disease has spread.

Remember!

When we write newspaper articles about factual events, we want to fully inform the readers about a situation. This means that we have to include details about who was involved, what happened, where, when and how an event happened.

Newspaper articles always have a headline and usually have language features such as direct speech, reported speech and the passive voice.

Model writing task

Read the writing task and the model article and write who, what, where, when or how next to the highlighted parts. Then find examples of direct speech, reported speech and the passive voice.

Write a newspaper article about a crime involving a young person.

model composition

Youth sentenced for armed robbery

who
A 15-year-old boy is tonight beginning a three-year sentence for armed robbery. The youth, who cannot be named, robbed a post office in Battersea two months ago. Using a knife, he forced post office employees to put £700 into a suitcase. Police arrived on the scene just as he was attacking one of the employees. The thirty-two-year old was slightly injured and had to be taken to hospital.

Judge Chris Kelly said as he announced the sentence, 'This is the fourth time you have appeared in my court. Despite previous warnings and home detention, it seems that you have chosen a life of crime. Due to the seriousness of your latest crime, I have no option but to give you the highest sentence possible: three years at Carlton Young Offenders Institution.'

The boy's mother later commented that although she was shocked by her son's actions, she felt her son had been treated unfairly. She added that the maximum sentence of three years was too strict for a 15-year-old.

An eyewitness who provided evidence during the boy's trial said, 'I'm glad he's been sentenced. The robbery was one of the most terrifying experiences of my life. I'll never forget it.'

A court spokesperson later commented that in spite of the establishment of programmes to reduce youth crime, there has been an increase in the last year. She claimed that 589 youths had appeared in court this year, whereas last year's figure was only 422.

Grammar

A Circle the correct words.

1 Even although / (though) it was her first crime, she was sent to prison.

2 In spite / Despite of previous warnings, they committed more crimes.

3 Although / Despite the bad weather, the rescue workers battled on.

4 The paramedic went into the building even though / in spite it was on fire.

5 In spite of the fact that he was / being a trained police officer, he felt scared.

6 Although / Despite she felt fine, they rushed her to the hospital.

B Tick (✓) the correct sentences and correct any errors.

1 She was given a warning despite the fact having committed previous crimes.

She was given a warning despite having committed previous crimes.

2 Although he hadn't finished his basic training, he had to fight the fire.

_____

3 They dumped the rubbish even though the sign saying it was illegal.

_____

4 In spite of all the necessary measures had been taken, the crowd went out of control.

_____

5 An eyewitness said that despite it being a windy day, the forest fire hadn't spread.

_____

6 She ignored the cry for help, although the fact she was on duty.

_____

Your writing task

A Read the writing task and complete the plan with ideas for your article.

Write a newspaper article about a crime that has been committed in your area.

Headline: _____

Paragraph 1: Introduce the crime and give basic details about who (_____),
what (_____), where (_____),
when (_____), and how (_____) it happened.

Paragraph 2: Give more details about the crime and its consequences.

Paragraph 3: Provide an eyewitness account.

Paragraph 4: Provide a comment by a spokesperson.

Paragraph 5: Conclude the article and make a general comment about the crime in general.

B Now write your article.

Reading

A Read the article about mountain rescue.

All in a day's work

When most people say they had a hard day at work they normally mean they had too much to do, they had an argument with a colleague or customer, or their boss complained about their work. For others, it means that they have risked their lives in order to save others.

For some people the idea of a perfect day is one spent doing extreme sports like rock climbing up a mountain. However, what happens when their perfect day turns into a bad day due to an accident or getting lost? That's when they have to rely on those whose vocation in life is to save others at all costs.

Mountain rescue workers are highly-trained professionals or volunteers. Whether they take part in rescue missions to earn a living or not, they all get a great deal of satisfaction out of helping people in need. As well as being experienced climbers, rescue workers must be able to give first aid to any casualties they rescue. This may involve treating wounds, preparing a broken arm or leg or keeping people warm until they can be moved to safety.

In England and Wales, the Mountain Rescue Committee was set up following serious climbing accidents at the beginning of the twentieth century. Today, it has 3,500 volunteers who are on stand-by 24 hours a day, every day of the year. The volunteers' duties have been broadened in recent years to include various activities in cities. These are things like searching for people who have gone missing and helping to rescue victims of natural disasters such as floods.

Finally, rescue workers also help police investigating crimes. They are often called upon to search huge areas of countryside for evidence when a serious crime has been committed. The rescue workers are used to open country and searching in dangerous conditions. In addition, they are also asked to help preserve crime scenes until a full investigation can be conducted and all relevant evidence gathered.

It seems the value of mountain rescue cannot be underestimated. They have proven that they are essential to society in general and not just to those who practise risky leisure activities.

B Answer the questions.

1 Why might an ideal day not turn out as planned for extreme sports enthusiasts? _Because they may have an accident or get lost._

2 What do all mountain rescue workers gain from their job? _____

3 What skills must mountain rescue workers have? _____

4 Why do mountain rescue workers sometimes have to work in urban areas? _____

5 How do mountain rescue workers help the police investigate crime? _____

Vocabulary

Choose the correct answers.

1 During a recession everyone has to _____ .
  a tackle
  b monitor
  c (economise)

2 They used _____ to open the crashed car's door.
  a a tool belt
  b cutting equipment
  c goggles

3 The civil engineer will show us the _____ for the house later.
  a establishment
  b blueprints
  c overalls

4 He got the casualty to stay _____ so he could treat her.
  a still
  b on duty
  c on stand-by

5 There has been a _____ at the house next door.
  a fine
  b burglary
  c hazard

6 Never play _____ on the emergency services.
  a tricks
  b ropes
  c false alarms

7 We must _____ the village immediately.
  a flock
  b conduct
  c evacuate

8 _____ is essential in dealing with emergencies.
  a Co-ordination
  b Application
  c Detention

9 Helen has _____ on a first aid course.
  a graduated
  b enrolled
  c applied

10 Arson is a form of _____ .
  a crime
  b hoax
  c vocation

11 They _____ the shoplifter red-handed.
  a caught
  b declared
  c hired

12 She was taken to _____ on charges of blackmail.
  a estate agents
  b court
  c investigation

Grammar

Choose the correct answers.

1 The police officer _____ that he would shoot the thief.
  a (threatened)
  b begged
  c refused

2 He took the job _____ it wasn't what he wanted.
  a despite
  b in spite
  c even though

3 The judge _____ given new information about the case yesterday.
  a is
  b was
  c has been

4 The spokesperson said that an investigation would _____ conducted.
  a to be
  b be
  c being

5 The paramedic told me _____ .
  a to not panic
  b don't panic
  c not to panic

6 She _____ that she had graduated the previous year.
  a told
  b said to
  c said

7 They asked _____ they could have the afternoon off.
  a what
  b whether
  c who

8 His house had been burgled the day _____ .
  a before
  b previous
  c following

9 The police officer asked _____ had been stolen.
  a if
  b who
  c what

10 I'm pleased at _____ asked to go for a second interview.
  a having been
  b to be
  c be

11 Despite _____, they stayed in their home.
  a the fact a flood
  b it had flooded
  c the flooding

12 The building _____ being evacuated at this moment.
  a is
  b should
  c has been

Vocabulary

A Complete the crossword puzzle.

Across

2 John is going to _____ a new song on his guitar.

5 A _____ is a very successful film.

6 _____ refers to a special beauty or charm.

Down

1 A _____ is something that makes a situation difficult.

3 A _____ is a woman who makes clothes.

4 An _____ is a place where children who don't have parents grow up.

Crossword grid letters: 1 Down starting C-O-M-P-L-I-C-A-T-I-O-N; 2 Across starting C; 3 Down S; 4 Down O; 5 Across B; 6 Across G

B Choose the correct answers.

1 The film _____ the story of one of the most famous fashion models.
   - (a) tells
   - b limits
   - c makes

2 Do you think that designer is _____ of his time?
   - a ahead
   - b designed
   - c composed

3 He does his best to achieve _____ in his work.
   - a attitude
   - b designer
   - c perfection

4 Just because you work in the fashion industry doesn't mean you're _____ .
   - a superficial
   - b limited
   - c cynical

5 He had to _____ the song as he went along.
   - a improvise
   - b complicate
   - c design

6 I love _____ music and classical music.
   - a realistic
   - b stereotypical
   - c mainstream

C Match.

1 There are numerous

2 They have made a name

3 Despite its limitations,

4 The plot was too complicated

5 The dance routine wasn't rehearsed;

a to follow.

b it was an improvisation.

c books about the fashion business.

d for themselves in green energy.

e the play was a huge success.

Grammar

A Look at the pictures and write T (true) or F (false).

1   They're all wearing stripy, short-sleeved T-shirts.   ☐ F
2   The red apple isn't as big as the green apple.   ☐
3   The man on the left is taller than the man on the right.   ☐
4   She has got short, curly, blond hair.   ☐
5   She looks focused on what she's doing.   ☐
6   They're older than most pianists.   ☐

B Put the words in the correct order to make sentences.

1   short / Rosa / Italian / is / seamstress / thin / the
    <u>Rosa is the short, thin, Italian seamstress.</u>

2   practises / less / worse / he / the / gets / the / he
    _____

3   successful / film / expected / wasn't / as / we / the / had / as
    _____

4   most / he / the / of / dress / all / beautiful / designed
    _____

5   ordered / coat / long / a / blue / I / silk
    _____

C Answer the questions.

1   Which singer do you think is the trendiest?
    _____

2   What does your favourite item of clothing look like?
    _____

3   What is more important to you, clothes or music?
    _____

4   What makes you angry?
    _____

Vocabulary

A Match.

1	busking	c	4	tambourine	☐
2	accordion	☐	5	clarinet	☐
3	bass drum	☐	6	dress rehearsal	☐

B Complete the word groups with these words.

bagpipes   element   glory   ~~percussion~~   uplifting

1	wind	string	_percussion_
2	clarinet	flute	_____
3	moving	inspiring	_____
4	success	triumph	_____
5	part	aspect	_____

C Choose the correct words.

1 All the musicians are on stage for the _____ .
   a   songwriter
   (b) sound check
   c   lyrics

2 They all _____ into song without rehearsing.
   a   broke
   b   told
   c   sang

3 Greek music is extremely _____ with lots of styles and kinds of instrument.
   a   spontaneous
   b   varied
   c   planned

4 Can you pass _____ the song sheets, please?
   a   up
   b   by
   c   around

5 He never passes up the _____ to play his guitar.
   a   chance
   b   indication
   c   event

6 Music traditions are often passed _____ from one generation to another.
   a   up
   b   through
   c   down

Grammar

A Rewrite the sentences with the adverbs in brackets in the correct place. Sometimes more than one answer is possible.

1 They played the song. (loudly)

<u>They played the song loudly.</u>

2 We're going to the fashion show. (tomorrow night)

3 She fell off the stage. (nearly)

4 He left the guitar. (over there)

5 The models were exhausted. (absolutely)

6 They sang the song. (spontaneously / at the party)

B Match.

1	Our seats were the	a	to play outside?
2	They quickly learnt the lyrics	b	outside the studio.
3	Is it too hot	c	at the hotel last night?
4	They aren't dedicated enough	d	as he could to find a new singer.
5	He tried as hard	e	furthest away from the stage.
6	Did the group arrive	f	to become serious musicians.

C Tick (✓) the correct sentences and correct any errors. Sometimes more than one answer is possible.

1 She wrote the address on her music score quickly. _____✓_____

2 The audience screamed throughout the concert loudly. _____

3 They ran outside as fast as they could. _____

4 He put the dress yesterday carefully into the case. _____

5 The video clip was so badly made, we decided not to use it. _____

6 They broke into song in the playground cheerfully. _____

Vocabulary

Write M (materials), C (clothes), F (feelings) or S (size).

1	dreamy	☐ F	
2	patent leather	☐	
3	bow tie	☐	
4	tuxedo	☐	
5	thoughtful	☐	
6	huge	☐	
7	baggy	☐	
8	denims	☐	

9	suede	☐
10	tiny	☐
11	velvet	☐
12	slender	☐
13	silk	☐
14	halter-neck top	☐
15	confident	☐
16	anxious	☐

Listening

A 🎧 **Listen to Scott and Lisa talking and change the words in bold to make the sentences true.**

1 The photo album was **lying on the sofa**.   _on the coffee table_

2 Scott and Lisa's parents seem **happier** in the photo.   _____

3 Scott's dad was **in favour of** Scott having long hair.   _____

4 In the photo, their mum's wearing a **tiny** hat.   _____

5 Their dad is wearing **long** denims in the photo.   _____

6 Scott wants his dad's **silk** shirt.   _____

B 🎧 **Listen to Lena and Anton talking about arrangements for a fashion show. Decide whether each statement is right (A) or wrong (B).**

		A	B
1	Lena and Anton first want to discuss which models to hire.	☐	☑
2	Lena persuades Anton it's best to finish the show with the wedding dress.	☐	☐
3	When the show begins, models will already be on the catwalk.	☐	☐
4	The male models will be wearing tuxedos at the end of the show.	☐	☐
5	Anton suggests that Carla wears suede shoes.	☐	☐
6	They agree to discuss music at 4.30.	☐	☐

Speaking

Remember!

When we are describing people's feelings we use expressions like these.

He/She looks/seems/appears to be afraid/anxious/cheerful/ confident/dreamy/guilty/indifferent/sad/thoughtful.

When we are describing size we use expressions like these.

He/She is very tall/small/of small/medium/large build/chubby/slender. It is big/huge/tiny/miniature.

When we are describing clothes and appearance we use expressions like these.

He/She is wearing ...

He/She has got ... on.

He/She/It looks elegant/wacky/fashionable/trendy/ ridiculous/old-fashioned/uncomfortable/impractical.

A Complete the table with appropriate adjectives that could describe the people in the photos in C.

	Photo 1	Photo 2	Photo 3	Photo 4
Feelings				
Size				
Clothes/ appearance				

B Read the task in C and tick (✓) the things you might want to bear in mind when making your choice.

1 The cover should appeal to both girls and boys. ☐

2 The idea of spring should be obvious if possible. ☐

3 The photo must represent both fashion and music. ☐

4 There doesn't need to be a young person in the photo. ☐

5 The cover should look wacky. ☐

6 The cover should reflect young people's interests. ☐

C Imagine you and your partner work for a music and fashion magazine and have to decide on the front cover of the spring issue. Discuss these photos and choose which one you think is most suitable, giving reasons for your choice.

Discussion

'We shouldn't judge people based on their appearance.' Discuss.

Vocabulary

Circle the correct words.

1   These nowadays / (days) there are many dangers involved in modelling.

2   It is essential to get into the habit / focus of practising.

3   Besides the advantages, there are many drawbacks / benefits.

4   Let us look at / for why this situation has developed.

5   It not only appeals to children, and / but it also appeals to older people.

6   There are many benefits of listening / to listen to traditional music.

Remember!

Remember when we are writing an essay presenting advantages and disadvantages, we must write in an appropriate manner. The language that we use to discuss benefits is different to the language we use to describe disadvantages. When presenting positive ideas, we use the affirmative form of verbs; verbs like **improve**, **allow** and **create**; nouns like **advantage** and **benefit**; and positive adjectives and adverbs like **marvellous**, **happily** and **gladly**. When presenting negative ideas, we use the negative form of verbs; verbs like **harm**, **damage** and **prevent**; nouns like **disadvantage** and **drawback**; and negative adjectives and adverbs like **annoying**, **embarrassing**, **frustrating**, **terribly** and **unfortunately**.

Model writing task

Read the writing task and the model essay below. Circle the words and phrases used in favour of the argument and underline those used against the argument.

Write an essay discussing the advantages and disadvantages of getting music from the internet.

model composition

Nowadays, it is very easy to get access to your favourite music on the internet. It is no longer necessary to buy CDs from music shops. The question is, however, is this a good thing or not? Let us look at both the pros and cons.

There are undoubtedly many advantages of getting music from the internet. First of all, it tends to be cheaper than buying expensive CDs from shops which means that music fans save a lot of money. Also, fans can listen to music first and download whatever they really want to buy. They are able to do this in the comfort of their own homes at any time of the day.

However, there are also disadvantages of downloading music. Firstly, unless you are very experienced with a particular website, it sometimes takes too long to download each song. This means that music fans end up spending hours trying to find the music that they want, which is annoying. Another drawback is that it can cause small music shops to go out of business. If more and more people download from the internet then shops won't be able to survive.

To conclude, downloading music from the internet has many negative aspects. It can be very time-consuming and cause music shops to close. On the other hand, I feel there are more advantages than disadvantages as fans have more control over and pay less for the music they buy when they get it from the internet.

Grammar

A Complete the pairs of sentences with the correct words.

1 ~~interested~~   ~~interesting~~
   a   I didn't find the magazine at all _____*interesting*_____ .
   b   Are you _____ in coming to the concert tomorrow night?

2 **amused**   **amusing**
   a   The fans weren't _____ when the show was cancelled at the last minute.
   b   Jade found the comedian very _____ .

3 **terrified**   **terrifying**
   a   This report on the industry is _____ .
   b   The model is _____ of heights.

4 **embarrassed**   **embarrassing**
   a   We were _____ by Greg's behaviour.
   b   Katrina's singing was _____ .

5 **stunned**   **stunning**
   a   Lara's designs were _____ .
   b   Everyone was _____ when the models walked onto the catwalk.

B Circle the correct words.

1   These clothes are too big for her wear /(to wear).
2   Reading magazines is great / a great way to spend your free time.
3   Do you find listening to music relaxed / relaxing?
4   It's absolutely essential be / to be at the rehearsal on time.
5   It was one of the most thrilling / thrilled video clips ever.

Your writing task

A Read the writing task and complete the plan for your essay with the ideas in the box.

Write an essay discussing the advantages and disadvantages of young people having to pay for their own clothes.

> Discuss the advantages of young people buying their own clothes.
> Discuss the disadvantages of young people buying their own clothes.
> ~~Introduce the topic and say that there are advantages and disadvantages.~~
> Sum up the main ideas and state your opinion.

Paragraph 1:   *Introduce the topic and say that there are advantages and disadvantages.*
Paragraph 2:   _____
Paragraph 3:   _____
Paragraph 4:   _____

B Now write your essay.

Vocabulary

A Match.

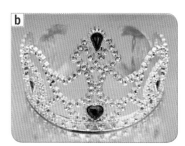

1 icing sugar ☐ f
2 maid ☐
3 mansion ☐
4 butler ☐
5 dresser ☐
6 tiara ☐

B Complete the paragraph with these words.

bottom	conclusions	hands	~~murder mysteries~~	rest	sleuth

One of my favourite genres of novel has always been (1) _____ murder mysteries _____ .
As a student I was a big fan of Nancy Drew and would read every one of her books I could get my
(2) _____ on. She was an amazingly talented young (3) _____
who would always try to get to the (4) _____ of any mysteries or crimes that
happened in her hometown of River Heights. No matter what the mystery was, Nancy was always on the case
and would never have a (5) _____ until the mystery was solved. Nancy would never
dismiss any clues as being unimportant. In fact, the secret of her success was recognising how all the little clues
could help her to draw the right (6) _____ . If you're looking for a good mystery, then
these books could be what you're looking for.

C Circle the correct words.

1 Was the dust on the dresser crumbling / (disturbed)?
2 The maid was biting her nails shortly / nervously.
3 She dismissed / sampled the water and said it tasted horrible.
4 Has anything out of the mind / ordinary happened lately?
5 The thief had concealed / crossed the jewels inside some curtains.

Grammar

A The words in bold are wrong. Write the correct words.

1 That bag isn't **herself**; it's mine!   _____hers_____

2 The children found **theirselves** a place to hide.   _____

3 She questioned absolutely **someone** connected with the crime.   _____

4 We solved the case all by **ours**!   _____

5 He blames **his** for leaving the money in the house.   _____

6 The mansion **its** was in a very bad condition.   _____

B Circle the correct words.

1 Did you hurt you / (yourself) climbing out of the window?

2 There wasn't anybody / nobody in the car.

3 Tell them not to touch the money; it's my / mine.

4 Something / Someone wasn't right with the butler's story.

5 He caught the criminals herself / himself without any help.

6 I blamed me / myself for the incident.

C Put the words in the correct order to make sentences.

1 go / ourselves / Stonehenge / let's / to
  Let's go to Stonehenge ourselves.

2 anything / saw / suspicious / no one
  _____

3 aren't / those / yours / stones
  _____

4 the / herself / plan / made / she
  _____

5 is / through / someone / looking / window / the
  _____

6 is / gun / his / the
  _____

Vocabulary

A **Match.**

1 Archaeologists are in agreement   a from us?

2 What did they use to make   b about the age of the stones.

3 We should always respect   c out in this region?

4 What secrets is the settlement keeping d our teachers.

5 In theory the mystery is easy to solve, but e the surface smooth?

6 When did those animals die   f in practice it is proving difficult.

B **Find six words and use them to complete the sentences.**

S	F	C	N	D	P	L	T	B	N
F	H	T	C	E	G	L	R	Y	O
P	S	D	S	P	M	O	I	A	K
U	P	C	T	I	A	P	V	X	M
Z	M	R	E	C	H	L	I	A	R
Z	L	U	R	T	F	B	A	Z	A
L	E	S	Y	M	B	O	L	I	C
E	O	C	C	U	P	A	N	T	S
U	G	R	A	C	E	F	U	L	E

1 The statue is very beautiful and _____graceful_____ .

2 The _____ of the village were all farmers.

3 What does this cave painting _____?

4 This ring wasn't worth much, but it was probably of _____ value.

5 I don't want to know the _____ details; tell me what's important.

6 The mysteries of the ancient world still _____ us today.

C **Write the missing letters.**

1 This is when one thing is joined to another.   a t t a c h e d

2 This is a technique that is used to make designs on rock and stone.   e _ _ _ _ _ _ _ _

3 This is somebody who makes something.   c _ _ _ _ _ _ _

4 This means 'huge'.   v _ _ _

5 This is something persuasive.   c _ _ _ _ _ _ _ _ _ _

6 This material was used in pre-historic times.   f _ _ _ _   s _ _ _ _

Grammar

A **Complete the sentences with the correct form of the verbs given and the tenses in brackets.**

1   _____Have_____ you ever
    _____noticed_____ anything strange in
    your area? (notice) (Present Perfect Simple)

2   The detective _____ in the
    dining room for an hour when we arrived. (wait)
    (Past Perfect Continuous)

3   Whoever _____ this statue
    was truly talented. (make) (Past Simple)

4   Thousands of people _____
    to Macchu Picchu every day. (travel)
    (Present Simple)

5   Scientists _____ the truth
    until they have all the pieces of the puzzle.
    (not reveal) (Future Simple)

6   They _____ the stones
    at the moment. (move) (Present Continuous)

7   I _____ through my
    telescope when I saw Mars.! (look)
    (Past Continuous)

8   They _____ the area
    properly and missed important clues.
    (not search) (Past Perfect)

B **Look at the pictures and write T (true) or F (false).**

1   The sun was shining brightly on the stones.   `F`
2   The camel will have walked past
    the pyramid soon.   ☐
3   The house had been abandoned.   ☐
4   He's telling the other boy a secret.   ☐
5   The trunk hasn't been filled.   ☐
6   There isn't going to be a storm soon.   ☐

C **Choose the correct answers.**

1   UFOs _____, so it must have been a plane or a helicopter
    you saw!
    a   aren't existing
    b   don't exist   (circled)
    c   haven't existed

2   We _____ working on the petroglyph when the accident
    happened.
    a   will be
    b   have been
    c   had been

3   In theory, they _____ the mystery by the end of the week.
    a   are solving
    b   will have solved
    c   will have been solving

4   The sleuth _____ up and down when I entered the room.
    a   was walking
    b   had walked
    c   walks

5   It never _____ my mind that she
    was hurt.
    a   was crossing
    b   had crossed
    c   crossed

6   We have been visiting the
    archaeological site _____ .
    a   at the moment
    b   for years
    c   soon

7   _____ they examining all the evidence?
    a   Are
    b   Have
    c   Do

8   Careful! That rock _____ fall on you!
    a   is going to
    b   will
    c   will be

Vocabulary

Complete the sentences with these words.

Halloween costume   kidnapping   murder mystery   optical illusion   sleuth   ~~vampire~~

1   I don't want to dress up as a _____ Vampire _____ .
2   The lines look the same but it's actually a(n) _____ .
3   Mum's making my _____ tonight.
4   Veronica Mars is a young _____ . She solves mysteries.
5   The book I'm reading is a(n) _____ .
6   Did you hear about the _____ of the people on the plane?

Listening

A 🎧 **Listen to three people in a book group talking about books they have read and complete the table.**

	Author	Type of book	Best feature
The Perfect Hoax	(1) ___David Jones___	(2) _____ mystery	(3) _____
What's Out There?	(4) _____	about (5) _____	(6) _____
Turn a Trick	(7) _____	about (8) _____	(9) _____

B 🎧 **Listen and complete the notes.**

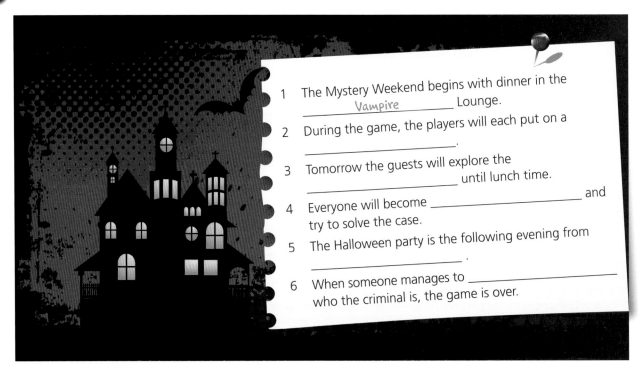

1   The Mystery Weekend begins with dinner in the _____ Vampire _____ Lounge.

2   During the game, the players will each put on a _____ .

3   Tomorrow the guests will explore the _____ until lunch time.

4   Everyone will become _____ and try to solve the case.

5   The Halloween party is the following evening from _____ .

6   When someone manages to _____ who the criminal is, the game is over.

Speaking

A Tick (✓) the words you associate with Halloween.

1. costume ✓
2. crop circle ☐
3. monster ☐
4. face painting ☐
5. mansion ☐
6. mask ☐
7. optical illusion ☐
8. prehistoric animals ☐
9. party ☐
10. mystery ☐

Remember!

When we are expressing preferences, we use expressions like these.

... is not particularly interesting/mysterious.

... is (un)suitable/(un)acceptable for young people.

... wouldn't go down well with ... because ...

... is by far the best choice because ...

... is the kind of thing young people go for/enjoy/like.

Young people would much rather + bare infinitive/prefer + full infinitive/noun ...

B Read the task in C and then complete the sentences about the pictures.

1 _____ isn't particularly interesting for a poster because _____ .

2 _____ wouldn't go down well with our friends because _____ .

3 _____ is by far the best choice because _____ .

4 Young people would much rather see _____ because _____ .

5 _____ is totally unacceptable for our party because _____ .

C You and your partner want to make a poster for a Halloween party at your school. Look at the pictures and discuss which two are most suitable for the poster.

Discussion

'People who wear costumes change their character.' Discuss.

Vocabulary

Match.

1   *Mysterious Day* was the most interesting film
2   The mystery begins when
3   I'd recommend the museum without
4   If you enjoy fancy dress parties,
5   I highly recommend the website

a   hesitation.
b   to anyone interested in crop circles.
c   I've ever seen.
d   you will love our end-of-term party.
e   a valuable painting goes missing.

Remember!

We use a qualifier before an adjective or adverb to increase its intensity. The qualifiers absolutely, completely, entirely, totally and utterly are extreme and can only be used with extreme adjectives and adverbs like amazing, awful, enormous, essential, excellent, freezing, furious, impossible and ridiculous. The qualifiers a bit, extremely, highly, rather, slightly, so, much and very can only be used with gradable adjectives and adverbs like angry, big, busy, disgusting, frightening, important, (un)likely, mysterious and recommended. The qualifiers fairly, pretty, really and quite can be used with both gradable and ungradable adjectives and adverbs.

Model writing task

Read the writing task and the model email and circle the correct words.

This is part of an email you received from an English-speaking friend.

> You told me in your last email that you were planning on visiting crop circles. What was it like? Would you suggest my sister and I go next year?

Write an email answering your friend's questions.

model composition

	Email				
New	Reply	Forward	Print	Delete	Send & Receive

Hi Sam,

Thanks for your email. It was (1) utterly / really great to hear from you again. I'm (2) completely / so glad you're thinking of visiting some crop circles. I'm (3) highly / absolutely sure you'll love them.

I went with my family in July and it was the most interesting tour we've ever taken. We travelled to Western Surrey where many crop circles appear every summer from around May on. Every year different shapes are made in the crops, but this year's were undoubtedly the most impressive ever. The talks by the guides were also (4) fairly / extremely fascinating. They told us everything about the history of crop circles and some (5) pretty / entirely mysterious tales people tell about them.

If you enjoy walking in the country and you don't mind travelling large distances to see unusual sites, you will love visiting the crop circles. I'm sure that you'll find them (6) totally / a bit amazing. I'll let you make up your own mind about how they were made, but I will say that I recommend the tour without hesitation.

If you do decide to go, let me know and I'll send you some (7) really / completely detailed maps and leaflets on the area, which are (8) absolutely / quite useful.

That's all for now.

Lots of love,

Dina

Grammar

A Complete the sentences with **so**, **such** or **such a**.

1 It was _____so_____ cold in the castle, I wanted to leave.
2 We had _____ good time solving the mystery.
3 There were _____ many books about the mystery in the library.
4 The detective is _____ careful, he never makes mistakes.
5 The Loch Ness Monster is _____ ridiculous story.
6 I've never seen _____ clever optical illusions.
7 Your Halloween costume is _____ scary!
8 It was _____ fascinating a mystery, I'd recommend the book.

B Circle the correct words.

1 There were so (many) / much people that we decided to leave.
2 She thought it was such / such a good idea that she couldn't wait to tell her friends.
3 He had so / such crazy ideas, we all thought he was mad.
4 The film was good, but it was so / such sad it made us cry.
5 So many / So much has been said about crop circles, I don't know what to think.

Your writing task

A Read the writing task and put the plan in the correct order by putting the paragraph number in the box.

This is part of an email you received from an English-speaking friend.

> You told me in your last email that you were organising a Halloween party. How did the party go? Would you recommend I try to organise something similar next Halloween?

Write an email answering your friend's questions.

Greeting: Hi (your friend's name),
Paragraph ☐3☐   Say whether you recommend your friend does something similar or not and give reasons.
Paragraph ☐   Bring the email to an end.
Paragraph ☐   Thank your friend for his/her email and mention the party briefly.
Paragraph ☐   Give details about the party and say whether it was fun or not.
Signing off: Lots of love, (your name)

B Now write your email.

Review 6

Reading

A Read the short articles about mysterious finds.

A Pre-Stonehenge buildings

The lands of southern England have long been associated with mystery. Pre-historic sites like Stonehenge are souvenirs from the past built by civilizations we still know very little about. An amazing discovery in June 2009, however, brought to light a whole complex that archaeologists didn't even know existed.

At first, archaeologists, who were carrying out routine research from a plane, thought they were looking down at crop circles. When they investigated more closely, they found that they were actually looking at circles that had been cut into the land. They were the marks of structures that existed around 6,000 years ago, before Stonehenge itself had even been built. The site was found in a village called Damerham which lies only 15 miles away from Stonehenge. The big question is, why did it take archaeologists so long to find it?

B Treasure trunk found

Terry Herbert, who's an amateur treasure hunter, got the surprise of a lifetime in July 2009. He was out looking for metal objects in farmland owned by a friend when he came across some gold. This led to the discovery of the largest Anglo-Saxon treasure trunk ever found. The treasure dates back 1,300 years to the time when England was divided into kingdoms. The treasure was found in what was once known as the Kingdom of Mercia, however the exact location is being kept a secret. The gold objects appear to have been decorations for weapons used in war. Who buried the treasure and when and why it was buried still remain a mystery.

C Bright smiles

In recent years, some people have had damaged teeth filled with gold. However, tooth jewellery is by no means a new trend. As far back as 2,500 years ago, Native Americans had their teeth decorated. Dentists at the time were very skilled at drilling holes through the teeth without damaging them in any way. They would then fill the holes with very colourful stones. Most of the people who had their teeth decorated were men. Researchers believe they did this purely because they thought it was attractive. It wasn't done to show how wealthy the person was. In fact, some of the wealthiest and most powerful people in this society had no decorations on their teeth.

B Write A (article A), B (article B) or C (article C). Which article...

1 doesn't say something was found by accident?   C
2 refers to something mainly linked to men?
3 discusses something discovered by professionals?
4 presents the oldest find?
5 deals with a strange fashion accessory?
6 mentions someone searching the ground for something specific?

Vocabulary

Choose the correct answers.

1 I prefer _____ trousers to tight trousers.
   - (a) baggy
   - b vast
   - c plentiful

2 The woman rudely _____ the maid.
   - a concealed
   - b dismissed
   - c complicated

3 She sat at the _____ and put on her jewellery.
   - a catwalk
   - b flute
   - c dresser

4 Bagpipes have got a _____ sound.
   - a luminous
   - b distinctive
   - c confident

5 I never _____ secrets from anyone.
   - a keep
   - b tell
   - c get

6 This desert is absolutely _____!
   - a vast
   - b smooth
   - c trivial

7 The shop specialises in wind instruments like the flute, the bagpipes and the _____ .
   - a accordion
   - b bass drum
   - c clarinet

8 The ballerina is such a _____ dancer.
   - a plaid
   - b distinguishing
   - c graceful

9 Don't forget, the dress _____ is at 7.30.
   - a rehearsal
   - b improvisation
   - c composition

10 _____ usually involves playing live music outside.
   - a Composition
   - b A sound check
   - c Busking

11 I prefer traditional music to modern _____ music.
   - a spontaneous
   - b stereotypical
   - c mainstream

12 The pattern creates an optical _____ .
   - a conclusion
   - b illusion
   - c confusion

Grammar

Choose the correct answers.

1 They _____ for clues for over an hour when I arrived.
   - a have been looking
   - (b) had been looking
   - c had looked

2 The design was _____ strange, no one liked it.
   - a such
   - b such a
   - c so

3 Can you have a look at these designs of _____?
   - a mine
   - b me
   - c myself

4 That's a _____ tiara.
   - a lovely, small, silver
   - b silver, lovely, small
   - c small, silver, lovely

5 This article on crop circles is _____ .
   - a fascinated
   - b fascinating
   - c most fascinated

6 This tambourine isn't _____ as a bass drum.
   - a heavier
   - b as heavy
   - c the heaviest

7 She hopes she will have enough money for the shoes _____ Friday.
   - a by
   - b since
   - c last

8 She walked _____ .
   - a last night onto the catwalk slowly
   - b slowly onto the catwalk last night
   - c onto the catwalk last night slowly

9 Unfortunately, _____ can replace the sick model.
   - a somebody
   - b anybody
   - c nobody

10 It was _____ show, we had to find extra seats.
   - a so successful a
   - b such successful
   - c so successful

11 He lives in the _____ mansion in the neighbourhood.
   - a more stunning
   - b most stunning
   - c most stunned

12 She always _____ the accordion beautifully.
   - a is playing
   - b plays
   - c has played

Crossword Puzzles

Units 1-2

Complete the crossword puzzle.

Across

4 This is the remains of a plant or animal that has become rock.

6 This is the opening of a film.

7 Things are on sale here.

9 This is like a test for singers, actors and dancers.

10 You do this when you say that something is true.

Down

1 This is a quick look.

2 This is another word for 'real'.

3 This person lives in a small settlement.

5 This describes something very beautiful.

6 You have this when you have the ability to achieve a lot in the future.

8 If something is this, you can see it.

Units 3-4

Complete the crossword puzzle.

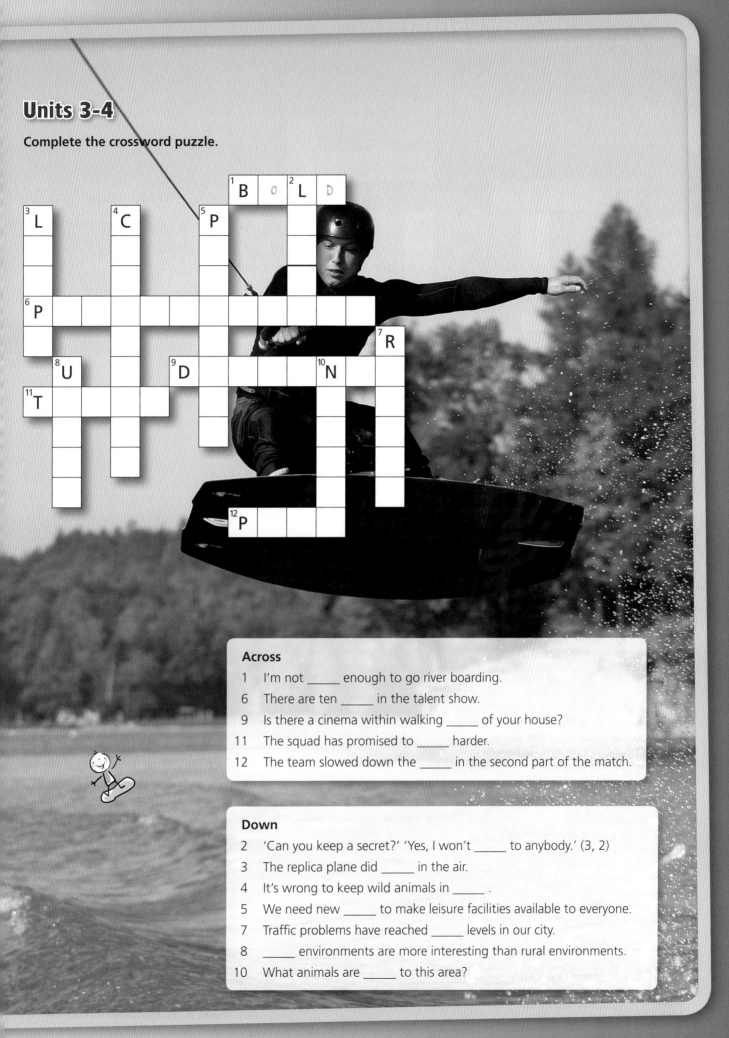

Crossword grid answers shown:
- 1 Across: B O L D
- 3 Down: L
- 4 Down: C
- 5 Down: P
- 6 Across: P
- 7 Down: R
- 8 Across: U
- 9 Across: D
- 10 Down: N
- 11 Across: T
- 12 Across: P

Across

1. I'm not _____ enough to go river boarding.
6. There are ten _____ in the talent show.
9. Is there a cinema within walking _____ of your house?
11. The squad has promised to _____ harder.
12. The team slowed down the _____ in the second part of the match.

Down

2. 'Can you keep a secret?' 'Yes, I won't _____ to anybody.' (3, 2)
3. The replica plane did _____ in the air.
4. It's wrong to keep wild animals in _____ .
5. We need new _____ to make leisure facilities available to everyone.
7. Traffic problems have reached _____ levels in our city.
8. _____ environments are more interesting than rural environments.
10. What animals are _____ to this area?

Crossword Puzzles

Units 5–6

Complete the crossword puzzle.

Across

2 How many oceans are there on the _____?
3 Dad doesn't drive a car, but he can ride his _____ .
7 You should always do a _____ before strenuous exercise. (4, 2)
8 Shall we walk up the stairs or take the _____?
10 I'm not going out to sea in this little _____!

Down

1 I'm very fit because I don't lead a _____ life.
4 Please _____ that you return all sports equipment to the cupboard.
5 Don't _____ on snacks! Have a proper meal.
6 This sea is full of _____ icebergs.
9 I didn't _____ to be a travel writer, but I became one. (3, 3)

Units 7-8

Complete the crossword puzzle.

Crossword grid letters:
- ¹D A T A B A S E
- ²I
- ³P
- ⁴E
- ⁵C
- ⁶L
- C
- ⁷E
- ⁸R
- ⁹G
- ¹⁰P

Across

3 You do this when you try to make somebody do something.

6 This is where rubbish is dumped.

7 You listen to music with these.

8 This is another word for 'fix'.

10 This is where you can look at the stars.

Down

1 Information is stored on this in a computer.

2 This is a new invention or idea.

4 A species that no longer exists is this.

5 You use this to take money out of a cash point. (4, 4)

9 This is a network.

Crossword Puzzles

Units 9-10

Complete the crossword puzzle.

```
¹T   ²O   B   □   □
     V
     E
     R            ³O
⁴H   R   H   □   □   □
□    A               □
□    L               □
□    L          ⁵V   □
     ⁶S  □  □  □  □  □  □  □
□              □     □
               □     □
          ⁷V   □
       ⁸C  □  □  □  □  □  □
               □
     ⁹B  □  □  □  □
               □
               □
```

Across

1 Can you pass my _____? I want to get my drill out. (4, 3)
4 The bricklayer put a _____ on her head before she went on the site. (4, 3)
6 Hannah's won a _____ to study at a private school.
8 There was only one _____ in the accident.
9 The fire engine rushed to put out the _____ .

Down

2 Put these _____ on over your clothes.
3 I can't do any more _____ at work this month.
4 This lamp is dangerous. It's a fire _____ .
5 He smashed our window and was charged with _____ .
7 Will there be a _____ at the office when Karim leaves?

118

Units 11-12

Complete the crossword puzzle.

Across

6   In this photo it looks like a part of the building is missing.
    It must be an optical _____ .

7   I can't get wait to get my _____ on the treasure.

8   The dog _____ the bone.

9   This desert isn't just big, it's _____ !

10 This picture _____ two horses.

Down

1   It never _____ my mind to question the children.

2   That model is both _____ and stylish.

3   The detective is _____ that he knows where the painting is.

4   The last inhabitants of the island _____ more than a thousand years ago. (4, 3)

5   She _____ this song for her new album.